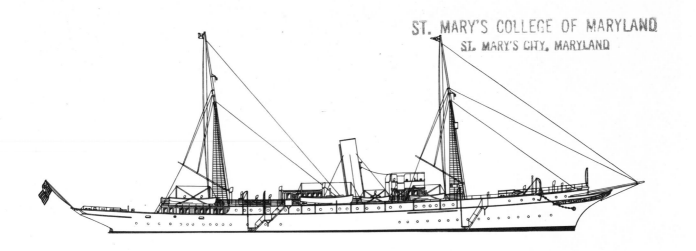

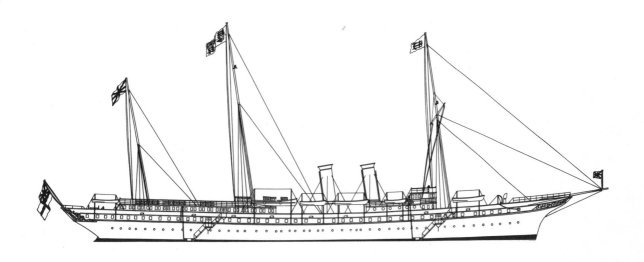

THE STEAM YACHTS

THE STEAM YACHTS

An Era of Elegance

by

ERIK HOFMAN

JOHN DE GRAFF, INC.
TUCKAHOE, N.Y.
1970

© Erik Hofman 1970
ISBN   0-8286-0040-6
Library of Congress Card Number: 73-96853

John de Graff Inc.
34 Oak Avenue
Tuckahoe, N.Y. 10707

TO
RONALD R. MOORE
Commander U. S. Coast & Geodetic Survey (ret.)

CONTENTS

INTRODUCTION

Time marches on. Things we take for granted suddenly fade away. Remember the tented circus, steam locomotives, trolley cars, coastal, bay and river steamers, distinctive automobiles? The disappearance of steam-powered yachts is a similar case. When I tried to get facts about these elegant relics of the past, there was a paucity of information. Furthermore, there are few people living with clear memories of steam yachts and their era. I am fortunate to have met and to have had generous help with data, photographs and memories from several enthusiasts. Ronald R. Moore, to whom this book is dedicated, is a retired Coast & Geodetic Survey officer. A civil engineer, he served on and commanded survey vessels. He started collecting data and photographs of steam yachts over 60 years ago. He made the drawings of individual yachts in this book. Without his encyclopedic knowledge, inspiration and cooperation, I doubt if I would have undertaken the task of preparing this book. L. Francis Herreshoff provided much from his technical experience as a yacht designer as well as from his unique position, growing up from childhood with the world of yachts as a son of Capt. Nat Herreshoff, the great yacht designer.

Among others in the USA to whom I am grateful are: W. A. Baker of MIT; Arthur Borden; H. E. Brown of Marine Research Society of Bath; Laurence A. Chappell Jr.; William M. Ewen; Robert Fuller; Sohei Hohri, Librarian of the New York Yacht Club; Edwin Littlefield formerly Chief Engineer of *Viking*; John Lochhead, Librarian, Mariners Museum, Newport News; H. S. Morgan; Charles Rodstrom; R. H. Rogers; Charles Schultz, Librarian, Mystic Seaport; Capt. Edwin Thompson, formerly of *Viking*; the U.S. Navy Dept. (Ships Historical Section).

In Great Britain, among others to whom I am indebted are: the late Frank Beken, photographer of Cowes, K. Adlard Coles; Capt. H. M. Denham RN (ret.); Major Desmond Dillon, Secretary Royal Yacht Squadron; John G. D. Henderson; George Naish, National Maritime Museum; John Nicholson; J. A. MacLachlin and William Smart of G. L. Watson & Company.

Finally, I am everlastingly indebted to John de Graff, who encouraged me to produce this book, and whose patience, and help has brought it into existence.

La Cabaneta
Mallorca, Spain
August 1969

1

KANAWHA GOING THROUGH THE FLEET

2

STEAM YACHTS—A HISTORY

The steam yacht was the most striking personal possession ever produced by man. It pronounced achievement. It publicized the millionaire as no other possession did. A stable of racehorses was displayed to comparatively few people at a track who saw an unknown being photographed under the nose of a handsome horse. A large estate and handsome house were hidden behind walls, the wealthier the owner, the higher the walls. A private railway car (in the United States) costing a mere bagatelle of around $50,000 was hidden on an obscure railway siding (except on the famous private car sidings at the old Royal Poinciana Hotel in Palm Beach where it was even more carefully guarded against intrusion by the hoi-polloi). The steam yacht, particularly in the United States, was there for everybody to see and envy, naturally at a distance. Anchored off New York City, moving on the Hudson River or on Long Island Sound, in full view of thousands, it served as a goal for the ambitious.

The steam yacht era has come and gone. It lasted for a mere 50 years; about 1864–1914 in Britain and about 1875–1917 in the United States, about the same era as the private railway car in the United States. Of course a few steam yachts were built before those dates and a few more were built after World War I.

There might have been one or more yachts with steam power in England in the 1820's since something must have been responsible for the Royal Yacht Club's resolution of May 5, 1827, which stated "the object of this Club is to promote seamanship to which the application of steam is inimical, and any member applying steam to his yacht shall be disqualified hereby and shall cease to be a member." Thomas Assheton-Smith, a prominent member of the Club, was so incensed at such an imposition on his personal possessions that he resigned from the Club in 1829 and built the steam powered *Menai* of 400 tons, the first yacht I can discover that was powered by steam in England. Pressure on the then-titled Royal Yacht Squadron resulted in another resolution in 1843 in which yachts powered by steam and owned by members of the Squadron would "have to consume their own smoke"! A further resolution in 1844 more logically permitted members to own yachts powered by steam engines of over 100 horsepower, and in 1853 all restrictions against steam were removed. In any case, 30 yachts powered by steam were listed in Britain in 1863, 140 in 1873, and 466 in 1883. In 1913, before losses and scrappings resulted from World War I, the number had dropped to 263. In 1938, before World War II reduced the number even further, only 193 steam powered yachts of any size were listed in Great Britain.

The first steam yacht race of record appears to have been held in 1868 between *Cornelia* and *Eothen*. As "it was hardly considered an improvement on the Squadron programme" it was not repeated.

In 1882, with more and more interest in racing cutters, it was stated that of all the cruising schooners and other cruising sailing craft owned by members of the Squadron, only 15 were not for sale. There were no regattas for cruising craft, and cruising members were shifting to steam, so much preferred for entertaining and by the ladies.

In the United States, the first steam yacht was probably the large (270' LOA-Length Over All) luxurious *North Star*, built for Commodore Cornelius Vanderbilt in 1853 and used by him on his memorable voyage to Europe and back that same year. The next known steam yacht was the *Firefly*, a 98' paddle steamer built in 1854 by Smith and Dimon for W. M. Aspinwall, then president of the Pacific Mail Steamship Co. *Clarita*, *Bijou*, and *Wave* followed in 1864. *Clarita* and *Bijou* were the first steam powered yachts registered in the New York Yacht Club yearbook of 1864. Herreshoff's first steamer (a 30' launch) was built in 1876. By 1913, 272 steam yachts over 75' LOA were listed in the American Lloyd's Register. In the New York Yacht Club yearbook of 1915, 169 steam yachts were registered in that club alone.

3

A tally of steam yachts registered in 1913 (and over 75' LOA to eliminate the hundreds of open steam launches) appears below. The year 1913 was selected since most large steam yachts were then in service and that year preceded the disappearance of many yachts due to losses and scrappings during World War I.

Countries	75–199' LOA or up to 499 TYM°	200–299' LOA or 500–999 TYM	300' & over or 1000 TYM & over	Total
United States	236	29	7	272
Canada	19	2	1	22
United Kingdom	210	41	12	263
France	34	7	2	43
Germany	8	0	1	9
Russia	5	4	3	12
Others	74	7	3	84
Total	586	81	29	696

° Thames Yacht Measurement. See Page 25.

STEAM YACHTS IN BRITAIN

Who were the owners of these large yachts in Britain? At first most of them inherited their wealth. As late as this century, one duke was reputed to have had an annual income of something like £4 million ($20 million). The present Duke of Bedford said his grandfather's (owner of *Sapphire*) annual income was well over £200,000 ($1 million) without income tax to pay. The Dukes of Sutherland and Westminster, both prominent yacht owners, were large land or property owners. The Rothschilds were, of course, bankers on an international scale, and had inherited the bases of their fortunes, though they themselves vastly increased their wealth. Lord Brassey inherited his wealth from his railroad contracting father, Colonel MacCalmont from an uncle. Lord Tredegar owned Welch coal properties. Owners such as Coats (thread), Guinness and Gretton (beer), Singer (sewing machines), and others inherited their fortunes from their illustrious, industrious ancestors. Shipping people such as Lord Runciman, Lord Pirrie, Lord Furness, and Lord Inchcape noticeably increased whatever fortunes they inherited. Among the few self-made yacht owners who generated really large fortunes were: Sir Thomas Lipton, who most acutely used his yachting and his America's Cup challenges to promote Lipton's tea; Gordon Selfridge of department store fame; S. B. Joel, of South African mines; and Sir George Newnes, the publisher. Later, in the diesel era, the "beerage," newspaper publishers, aircraft builders, and others became the owners of the newest and best yachts. Thomas Brassey, later Lord Brassey, was unique in that he was master of *Sunbeam*, and antedating any other yachtsmen by many years, was the first owner to obtain his yacht master's papers.

Thus steam yachting in Britain was limited, except for certain groups in recent years as noted above, to a comparatively small group of wealthy people, mainly of the nobility or large landowners. They could afford large, comfortable steam yachts. Many had had years of boating in sailing craft, or were of a generation that grew up accustomed to yachts. They accepted reasonable speeds, demanded seaworthiness, and, considering their yachts another home, had them fitted out in utmost comfort. Such people were of the leisured class, with plenty of time on their hands. Their lives were regulated by a "London season," a "race season," a "hunting or shooting season," a "fishing season," etc. In this grouping was Cowes week at which this class gathered under royal aegis. Spare time was available for cruising, though trips to Scotland for hunting or shooting or to Norway for fishing were often accomplished by yacht. Many would send their yachts to the Mediterranean for the winter (travelling overland to avoid the tempestuous Bay of Biscay), where they joined their yachts for cruising during the more pleasant winter months. They often used their yachts as floating homes while shooting on the Dalmatian and Ionian coasts. There would be 15–20 yachts based in Corfu. When one returned from a successful shoot she would, on anchoring, fire a cannon and "dress ship." However, instead of hoisting a string of flags to the mastheads, these yachts would "dress" with the game shot on the expedition.

There were few steam yachts of any size built after World War I. By that time, most of the new yachts were diesel powered. Several steamers such as *Lyndonia*, *Aloha*, and *Alcyone* were converted from steam to diesel. After World War II, two wartime steam reciprocating-engined frigates were converted to the yachts *Christina* and *Moineau*, while the British Royal Yacht-cum-hospital ship, *Britannia*, was built as new. These are the only known steam yachts that have appeared since that war. Even the 332' LOA (3110 TYM) yacht reported under construction in 1968 will be diesel powered.

The above table includes royal yachts, which comprised most of the large ones in Germany and Russia, and shows quite clearly the comparatively large number of big yachts in the United Kingdom (53 over 500 TYM against 36 in the United States) at that time. Some of the reasons for this are discussed later on. Though there were numerous small steam launches in those days, there was no large middle class of yachtsmen with powered (steam was the

4

only source of mechanical power) craft, as there is today. This class now constitutes the large majority of boat owners. In the steam yacht era, the comparatively few of this class who enjoyed boating did so in small sailing craft. Even cruising in sailing craft was quite limited before the early part of this century.

The era of the steam yacht follows, in some ways, that of the railroads. Development was not pressed. For many years there were only isolated cases of any real improvement in steam engine design. Herreshoff developed the steeple engine for yachts with a separate camshaft for valve operation, both of which shortened the engine and made it stiffer. He also pioneered enclosed crankcases that permitted splash lubrication. But in the main, engines remained of the tried and true triple expansion design. Eventually experimental diesel installations were made. They were, at first, costly, big, heavy, noisy, and very rough. Vibration was quite objectionable compared to the quiet, smooth steam engines. The saving graces of diesel engines at that time were their fuel economy and elimination of space for storing and handling of coal and ashes. However, diesel engine builders continued developing and improving their product, while steam engineers did little to improve their engines, especially in the smaller sizes. In the case of railroads, engineers belatedly started to develop new and improved designs, but they were handicapped by the limits on height and width of locomotives. In the marine field there was considerable development of big-ship turbines. Now, in the higher powers, turbines come closer to diesels in fuel economy and are smaller for equivalent powers, especially where, as in tankers, boilers are often located above the turbines, thus saving fore-and-aft space. But in yacht sizes such advantages do not equal those of smaller, higher speed diesels that are in volume production, and have improvements that reduce the noise and vibration of earlier designs. Furthermore, geared turbines show poor maneuvering characteristics, which can be accepted on the long runs of tankers and liners, but are objectionable on yachts where maneuverability is desired. Direct drive turbines are quite inefficient for ship propulsion.

Several builders of fine iron clippers turned to yacht construction as the clipper business succumbed to steam vessels. With their superior craftsmanship, too expensive for the commercial steamers, they could build the craft as designed by the technically trained yacht architects and as desired by the experienced owners. Thus, between the architects and the ex-clipper builders with their experience in good seaworthy craft, a series of British yachts evolved as seakindly, safe and reliable vessels, comfortable but not fast. Most of the early yachts were fitted with auxiliary sails as masters and crew were familiar with sail and were still distrustful of steam. Sails were often used for steadying the yachts, to assist them when on a reach, or in case of emergency, and the jibs at times were used to help cant and swing single-engined yachts when getting under way in tight places.

Owners, designers, and crews were reluctant to depart from the sailing ship appearance they were accustomed to, so clipper bows, bowsprits, jibs, masts with yards, and counter sterns decorated with gilded trailboards and counters were retained, often in modified form, for nearly the whole of the steam yacht era. Note the appearance of *Nahlin*, *Corsair* (4th), and *Viking* among the last of the steam yachts. Few modern yachts have the beauty of a clipper bow and bowsprit, of a graceful sheer, raking masts and funnels, and counter sterns. In the case of several, such as *Sunbeam*, and *Valhalla*, they were primarily sailing yachts with steam as auxiliary power. The greater part of *Sunbeam's* round-the-world voyage was done under sail. No effort was made to develop high power or high speeds on these yachts. The owners had all the leisure time in the world. As they were usually built to Lloyd's scantlings they were rather heavy, but steady. With their low pressure, heavy, fire-tube Scotch boilers and large, slow-turning, compound or triple expansion engines, they were very reliable. It is very seldom that one hears of a mechanical breakdown that was not fixed at sea by the vessel's engineers. As they were used for extended periods with Scotch boilers, in which fires could be banked, they did not have to be fast. They were first and foremost floating homes that could take them to distant places in comfort.

We in this present age often forget the limitations that existed in travel 70–100 years ago. Steam was the form of mechanical power. Airplanes had not been invented. Automobiles, though they were in existence, were unreliable, uncomfortable, and limited to the atrocious dirt roads that existed. Trains, except for the few private cars in the United States of America, were usually dirty, hot, and noisy. Private railroad cars could go only where railroads existed and could be "parked" only on out-of-the-way, disagreeable sidings or in train yards. Those interested in the opulence and splendor of private cars, whose era parallelled that of the steam yacht should read Lucius Beebe's "Mansions on Wheels." There was a similarity of ostentatious display between private cars and steam yachts in the United States of America, though regardless of ostentatiousness, the private car was limited to about 82' long × 10' wide × 14½' high with up to 5 tiny bedrooms, dining room, kitchen, crew room, and an observation lounge. Therefore, people who could, preferred to travel by water, particularly in Europe, so why not make the journey

5

Figure 1 Crew. *Cassandra* 1908

in comfort on one's own yacht, not to be tied to departures, routes, and arrivals.

Technical training for naval architects in the 19th century was generally more advanced in Britain, especially in Glasgow, than in the United States of America. So yachts built under their designs were more satisfactory, and less liable to mistakes. George L. Watson, whose firm is still active though he died in 1904, became THE great steam yacht designer with at least 60 to his name. He also was one of the great sailing craft designers, his *Valkyrie II* and *Shamrock II* often being conceded to have been better craft than their defending America's cup opponents. Watson's designs were not only seaworthy, comfortable, and reliable, their interiors were what owners wished, and his yachts were consistently beautiful. Only the third *Corsair*, designed by J. Beavor-Webb, could surpass some of Watson's designs for pure beauty. Many Americans, coveting a luxurious, comfortable floating home, would order from Watson or in the earlier days St. Clair Byrne. J. Beavor-Webb moved from England to the United States of America and designed several successful yachts. Cox & King was another well-known design firm.

As these yachts were frequently in commission the year round, they were able to select and retain a regular crew. Even if laid up, the principal officers and men would be kept at work on the yacht, overhauling boilers and engines, painting the hull and rig, etc. Yachts and local sailing vessels used in summers only usually had Essex or West Country fishermen, who would return to fishing during the winter season. They were very familiar with the waters they sailed in and the weather they encountered. Most steam yacht captains were experienced, serious professionals who had served in square-rigged ocean-going

craft or on steamship lines. They looked on their yachting as a career. As they could so often offer year-round employment, they could choose their deck crews and in time develop a smart, hard-working capable group. Captains and crews, of the larger yachts in particular, took great pride in outshining and being smarter than the various naval vessels they would meet, especially in the Mediterranean, where their owners and naval officers often exchanged visits and could make comparisons. Even so, life on board could be difficult if away for months at a time. Lord Brassey noted that the hands who had served on *Sunbeam* for some years formed, unconsciously perhaps, a clique of "old hands" who resented the newcomers and, with the artfulness of experience, shirked the more menial jobs.

The chief engineers were usually Scots, as most of these steam yachts were built and engined in Scottish yards such as Ramage & Ferguson, Ailsa, Stephen, Denny, Fairfield, and John Brown (Thompson). Many of these engineers had served their apprenticeship in those yards and often worked on the building of the engines they tended in service. Thus they had a thorough grounding in steam engine and boiler construction. These steam engines were largely hand built and finished. They were masterpieces of craftsmanship, hand turned, hand fitted, hand polished. Cylinder jackets were often made of polished and varnished costly woods. The whole engine-room staff took great pride in the spotless appearance of their engine rooms and spent a goodly part of their time polishing, shining, and painting their machinery. This same care was extended to commercial vessels. No matter how weathered a commercial vessel's exterior might be, the engine room was usually spick-and-span and shining. There doesn't seem to be quite

TABLE OF CREWS' WAGES

| Tonnage TYM | 1000 TYM Yacht | | 700 TYM Yacht | | 500 TYM Yacht | | 300 TYM Yacht | |
| LOA (est.) | 275' | | 225' | | 200' | | 180' | |
Costs	£ Sterl.	$ @ 5/£	£ Sterl.	$ @ 5/£	£ Sterl.	$ @ 5/£	£ Sterl.	$ @ 5/£
Cost of yacht	£50–55000	250–275M	£35–40000	175–200M	£25–28000	125–140M	£18–20000	90–100M
Deck Stores/month	£100	$500	£75	$375	£50	$250	£50	$250
Engine stores/month	£125	625	£80	400	£60	300	£55	275
† Coal for 1000 Mi./month	£76	380	£60	300	£163	815	£119	595
Wages/month	£372	1860	£246	1230	£24	120	—	—
Clothing/month	£41	205	£28	140				
Speed—Knots	13	—	12	—	11	—	12	—

† Coal costs assumed to be £1–1–0 per long ton at 2 lbs/SHP/hour + 30% for in port & extras.

WAGES/WEEK	*Fed by yacht.							
Captain (paid by the year)	* £6–£10	$30–50	£4–£5	$20–25	£4	20.00	£3–0	15.00
First Mate	* £3–0	15.00	£2–15	13.75	£2–10	12.50	£2–5	11.00
Second Mate	* £2–5	11.00	£2–0	10.00	£1–15	8.75	—	—
Boatswain	£1–10	7.50	£1–10	7.50	£1–10	7.50	£1–10	7.50
Carpenter	£1–15	8.75	£1–12	8.00	£1–10	7.50	£1–10	7.50
Quartermasters	4 x £1–9	4 x 7.25	2 x £1–9	2 x 7.25	2 x £1–9	2 x 7.25	—	—
Launchman, Gunner, B'sn Mate, Winchman	4 x £1–9	4 x 7.25	—	—	—	—	—	—
A B Seaman	8 x £1–6	8 x 6.50	8 x £1–6	8 x 6.50	4 x £1–6	4 x 6.50	6 x £1–6	6 x 6.50
Boy Seamen	£0–15	3.75	—	—	—	—	—	—
Ch. Engineer (paid by year)	* £5–0	25.00	£4–0	20.00	£3–6	16.50	£3–0	15.00
Second Engineer	* £3–10	17.50	£2–12	13.00	£2–10	12.50	—	—
Third Engineer	* £3–0	15.00	£2–0	10.00	—	—	—	—
Launch Engineer	£1–10	7.50	£1–10	7.50	—	—	—	—
Creasers	4 x £1–10	4 x 7.50	2 x £1–10	2 x 7.50	£1–10	7.50	—	—
Firemen	8 x £1–8	8 x 7.00	4 x £1–8	4 x 7.00	3 x £1–8	3 x 7.00	3 x £1–8	3 x 7.00
Ch. Steward	* £3–15	18.75	£2–0	10.00	£2–0	10.00	£1–15	8.75
Second Steward	* £1–15	8.75	£1–15	8.75	£1–10	7.50	—	—
Bedroom Steward	* £1–15	8.75	2 x £1–10	2 x 7.50	£1–10	7.50	£1–5	6.25
Cabin Boy	* £0–15	3.75	—	—	—	—	—	—
Officers' Steward	* £1–5	6.25	£1–5	6.25	£1–5	6.25	—	—
Owner's Cook	* £2–15††	13.75	£2–10	12.50	£2–0	10.00	£2–0	10.00
Officers' Cook	* £1–6	6.50	—	—	—	—	—	—
Pantryman	* £1–10	7.50	—	—	—	—	—	—
Forecastle Cooks	2 x 1–8	2 x 7.00	£1–10	7.50	£1–6	6.50	—	—
TOTAL	£87	435.00	£56–17	284.25	£38–4	191.00	£27–18	139.50

†† When owners cook was a "chef" wages were often far higher.

the same pride in diesel engine rooms, though admittedly the modern diesel does not provide the same expanse of machined parts for shining. There was apparently little standardization of parts of steam engines. Each one seems to have been individually built. Stresses pressures, and loads were comparatively low. Weight was not a limiting factor. Thus maintenance and repairs could be, or had to be, made aboard by simple machine tooling. Total breakdowns were practically unheard of. The majority of these yachts were single screw.

The stewards and their department constituted a most important part of the crew of a large yacht since, with the exception of the captain, they were most in touch with the owners and guests. They were the link between the floating and the permanent home. Owners and guests expected the same service and food on board as they were accustomed to receive ashore. Often members of the family household, especially ladies' maids or nannies, would move on board with the family, and life would continue as it had ashore. *Sunbeam*, on her round-the-world voyage, had four stewards, two cooks for the afterguard, as well as a nanny (for three children), a ladies' maid, and a stewardess. Figure 1, a view of the crew of the American yacht *Cassandra*, shows 11 in the stewards department and 31 others among the officers and men.

Stewards had an unenviable task before them to provide food of the type and variety the owners and guests were accustomed to ashore. There was little refrigeration or cold storage until the latter part of the era, so the steward and cook would have to purchase supplies in ports as they went along, dealing with the problem of strange languages, strange foods, and in the Mediterranean, heat and food spoilage. Luckily, perhaps, the English household of that era was not accustomed to refrigeration or ice-cold items except wines and champagne, so they could accept items purchased in their natural state. Ice was picked up wherever possible. It was a long time before ice-making machinery or mechanical refrigeration found itself on British yachts. The American yacht *Electra*, built in 1884, was famous primarily for her ice-making machinery, all 56 pounds of it per day, hardly enough to cool the champagne. Thus an experienced and imaginative Chief Steward would make the difference between a happy yacht and a sad one.

Crews on British yachts, as well as those on commercial vessels and workers in industry, were paid very low wages. In addition, except for the principal officers and those of the stewards department who came in contact with the afterguard, the crew had to provide their own food at their expense. The owner generously provided a forecastle cook who catered to the crew. Later, of course, the vessel fed all hands. Herbert Julyan says that the easiest crew to feed that he knew of was the Indian crew of the *Star of India*. Everyday a live sheep was pushed down the forecastle hatch, after which not a scrap of any kind appeared from below.

To indicate the costs of manning and operating yachts in those days the tables on page 7 are quoted from Dixon Kemp's "Manual of Yachting and Boat Sailing and Architecture," 1913 edition. The first three columns come from data that G.L. Watson & Co. provided to prospective clients. The last column, probably for yachts too small for Watson to be concerned about, is from Dixon Kemp himself. Those marked with an ° asterisk are the crew members enjoying food provided by the vessel. Please try to imagine how well the crew must have been fed on that part of 30 shillings per week total pay that they could afford for food.

The interiors of steam yachts varied from formally simple to some of the most luxurious, opulent interiors imaginable. Figure 2 shows the library and staircase of *Niagara* (1898, 272′ LOA, 1441 TYM). Other contemporary illustrations show clearly the apalling mass of Victorian bric-a-brac and what-nots found on yachts of that era to make them resemble parlors ashore. How stewards were able to keep these clean, and how they avoided wholesale breakage when the yachts rolled, as they did, defies the imagination. Even *Sunbeam*, a vessel normally at sea, and owned by one experienced in the movements that might be expected in a seaway, was littered with these objets d'art (page 38).

Valiant was a British-designed yacht built without regard to expense in 1893. A contemporary description of her interior demonstrates the splendor of yachts' interiors in those days, so different from the veneer or Formica panelling and plastic or fiberglass fabrics of today. Her 20 staterooms, salon, and library were decorated and furnished by a leading house in Paris. Some unpublished notes describe her interior.

"The salon, Louis XIV in style is panelled in fine grained French pine resembling English poplar, in white enamel with a gold finish. Every foot of the walls is of high relief, carved panelling of solid wood. At one end is a rich toned Steinway piano. Slender chairs, settees and a sideboard are Chippendale in design, with inlaid brass and upholstered in crimson silk velvet. The stained glass dome of the salon rises to the upper deck.

"A 100 ft. richly carpeted passageway connects the salon with the library, which too, is panelled in carved solid, dark walnut. Its furniture is solid carved walnut. Its carved walnut ceiling is chastened with paintings. Its fireplace of glazed brick has an exquisitely carved marble mantel. Bookcases have panelled doors with bevelled glass.

"The bedroom in the owner's suite below is rich but chaste. Sheraton in style it is painted ivory white flecked with gold and its draperies are of rich rose-colored flowered silk. The large carved bed is similarly enamelled and has matching covers. The adjoining bathroom has all copper piping. The owner's sitting room is Adam in style in carved dark mahogany with draperies of an unusual flowered green silk. Another owner's cabin forward has its ceiling, friezes and arches covered with a specially made Tynecastle tapestry decorated a rich ivory white. The walls are panelled with a light blue overstripe and floral designs of rich French silk. His after stateroom (the owner must have been a busy man) is exceptionally luxurious, panelled in figured Poland oak. Upholstery is a rich cream colored background and floral design of French silk, the canopied bed of the same oak is elaborately carved. Its ceiling friezes and arches, as in the forward cabin, are covered with specially woven tapestry. A blue carpet contrasts with the ivory tapestry. Ports are draped with silk curtains. Opening off this room, through a pair of richly carved doors is an elaborately fitted bathroom and lavatory. Adjacent is the private secretary's room in figured Spanish mahogany.

"Guests rooms are similar in magnificence, usually Spanish mahogany panelling with different colors and patterns of colored silk and tapestries. Bathrooms have all conveniences. The social hall is of elaborately carved fumed oak and furnished in rich red silk damask. The smoking room is panelled in carved Spanish mahogany. The main stairway and deck house are panelled in highly polished teak." Who wouldn't go to sea in such splendor?

Figure 4 shows the plans of *Margarita*, a typical

Figure 2 Library and staircase of *Niagara*

9

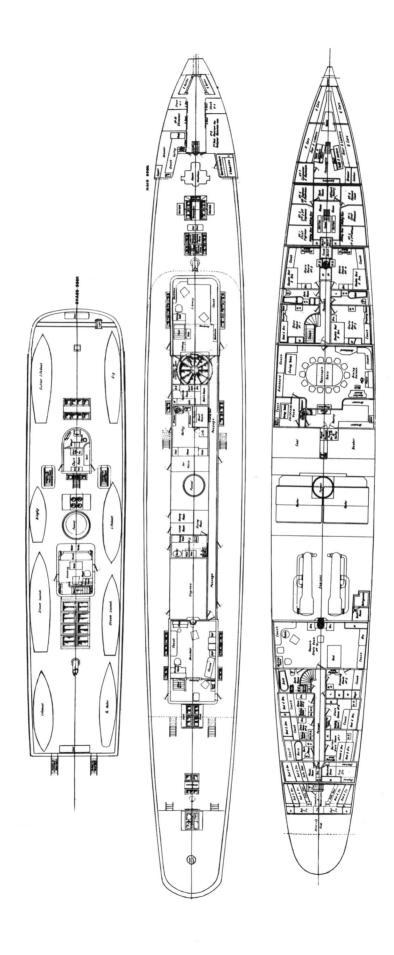

Figure 4 Deck plans. *Margarita* 1896

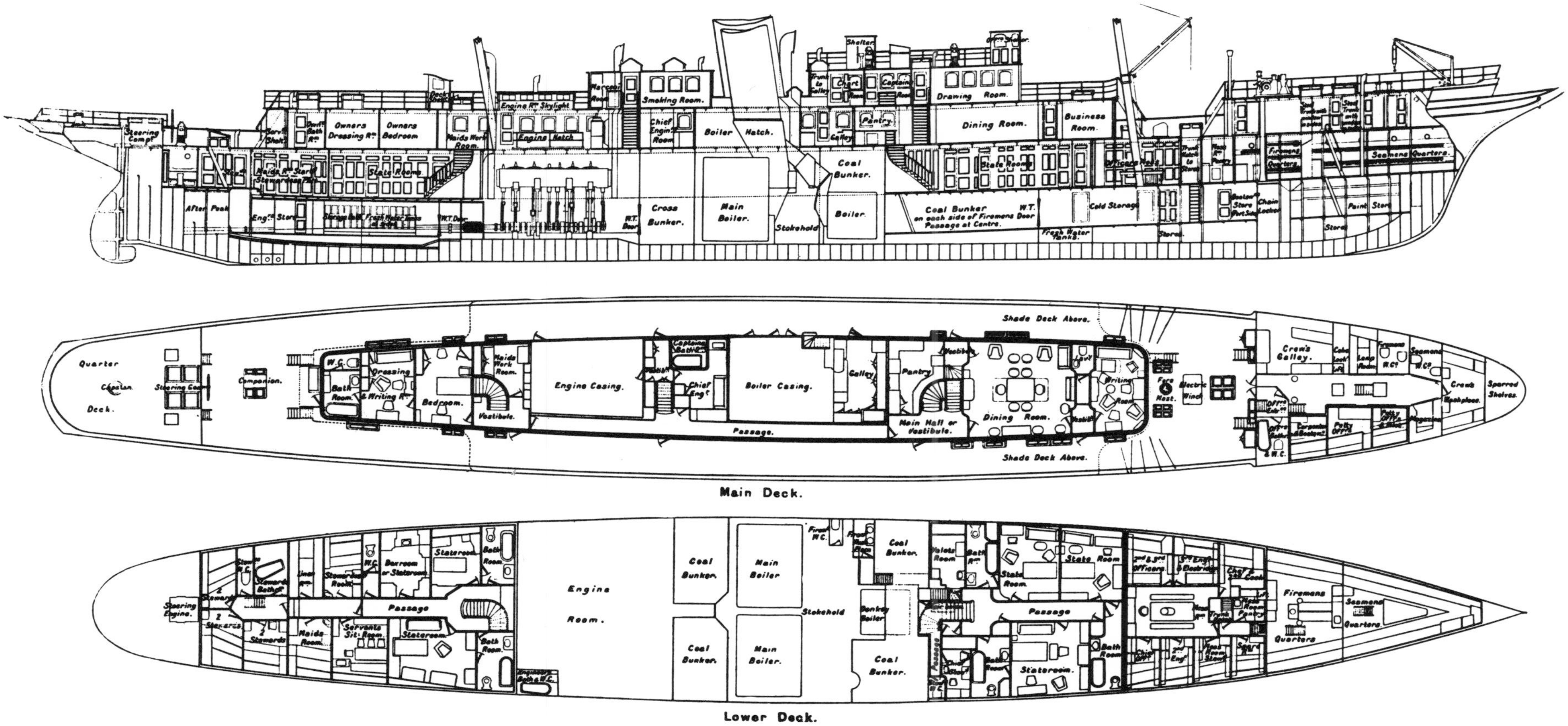

Figure 5 Profile plan and deck plans. *Sapphire* 1912

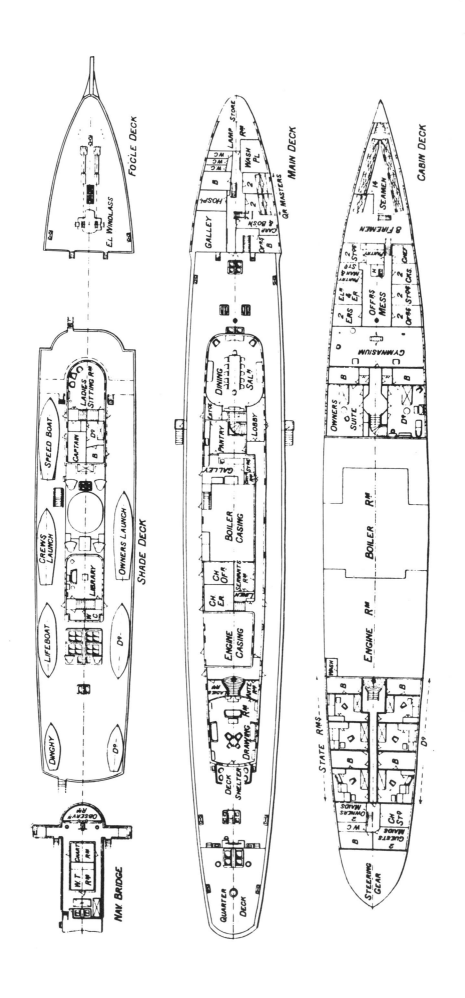

Figure 6 Deck plans. *Nahlin* 1930

12

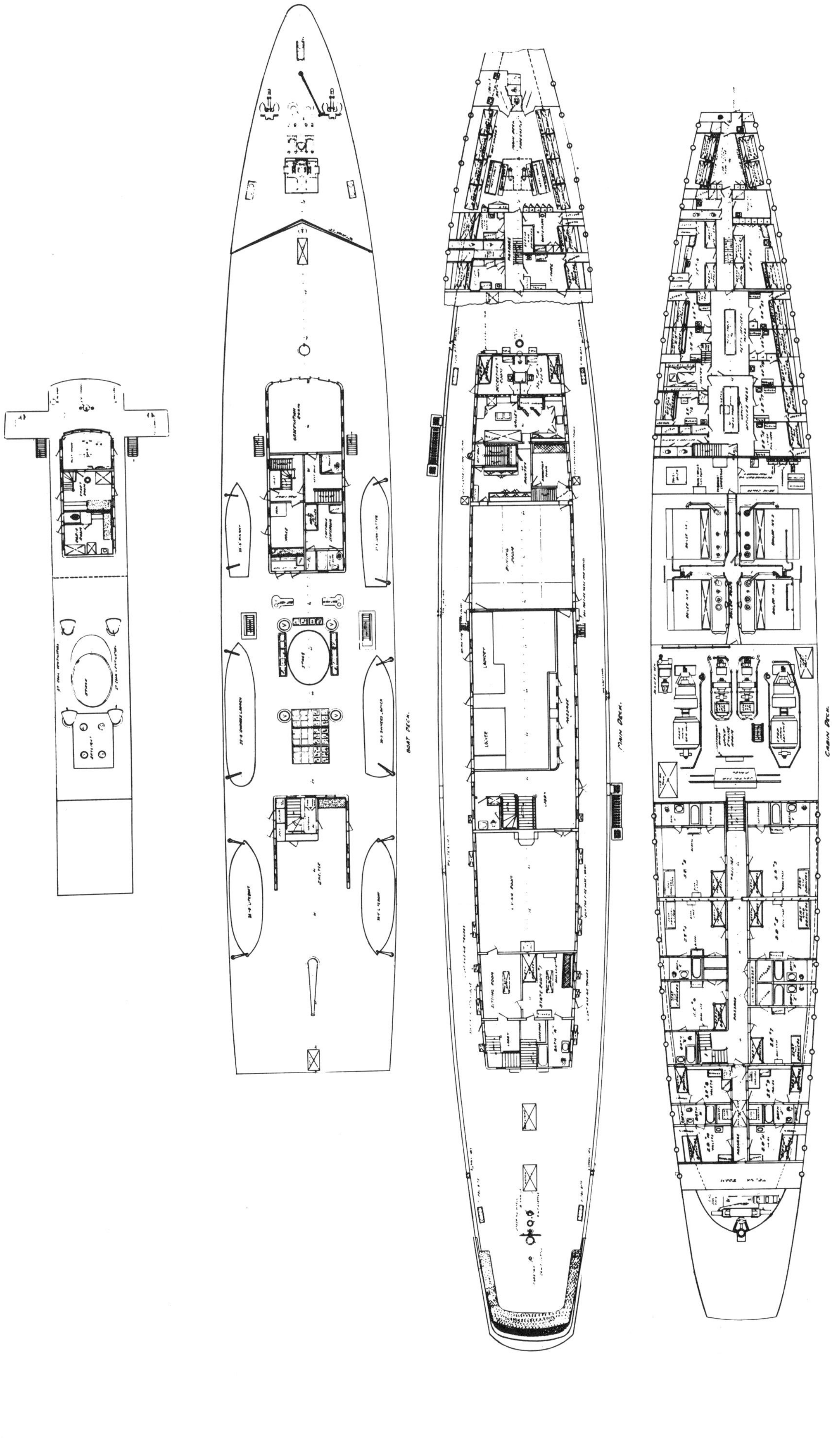

Figure 7 Deck plans. *Corsair* (4th.) 1930

13

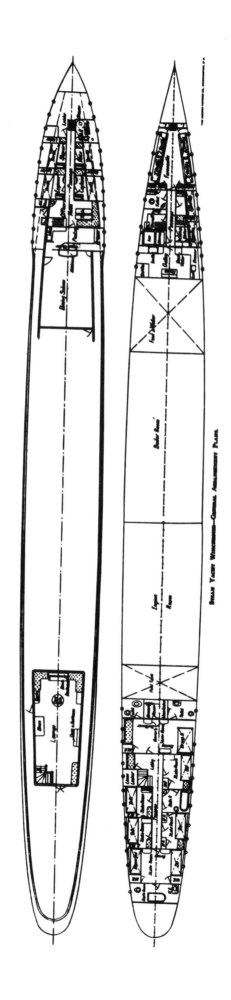

Figure 8 Deck plans. *Winchester 4th.* 1915

Watson design of 1896. Note that on 278′ LOA she could accomodate a large owner's cabin, four other good-sized cabins and three quite small cabins for the guests. Of course rooms were provided aft for the doctor as well as for the stewards, maids, etc.

Figure 5 shows the plan and interior profile of *Sapphire*, built in 1912 to G. L. Watson's designs. These drawings show a typical ocean-going steam yacht, yet one developed from the great many designed by the office of George Watson & Co. There are few improvements over the layout of *Margarita* built 16 years before. It is interesting to note not only the large space allotted to the crew, but the almost one third of the owner's quarters comprising stewards' and maids' rooms, their bathrooms, sitting room, and work room. Such owners travelled on their extensive voyages in comfort and were served as they were accustomed to at home.

Figure 6 shows similar plans of *Nahlin*. *Nahlin* was one of the last of the great steam yachts, and one of the last designed by that most experienced firm of G. L. Watson. One can study her layout confident that it was probably the finest of the 1930's. Lady Yule, her original owner, made a few extensive voyages, and before *Nahlin* was sold to the Roumanian Government, she was frequently chartered. (The most publicized charter was that to the new King Edward VIII who had her in the Mediterranean.) In *Nahlin* we can see the latest design thoughts in Britain. Even so, only two moderately large owner's cabins and six small guest cabins were accomodated in one of the most modern and beautiful steam yachts of the post-World War I era. Figure 7 shows the deck plan of the fourth *Corsair* built the same year for a most experienced and exacting American yachtsman who was assisted by his captain of many years' service in her design and layout.

STEAM YACHTS IN AMERICA

American yachts were, in general, rather different from British ones. Conditions of their employment were quite different. First, there were few people of the leisured class. Even J. Pierpont Morgan, who used his *Corsairs* more extensively than did most other owners, was an extremely busy banker. So, a great deal of the time, yachts in the United States were used, not for extended cruises, but to transport their owners to and from their homes on the Hudson River or Long Island Sound, or for weekends or short visits to Newport and nearby resorts. For such reasons of time, and of ignorance of sea craft in general, there was a greater demand for speed without the least understanding of what demands on space, cost, and lack of seaworthiness were imposed on a yacht. Figure 8 shows the plan of *Winchester*

(4th). No words can describe the sacrifices that had to be accepted to achieve a few knots more in speed. *Winchester*, 225′ long, could only provide an owner's stateroom with bath, one double and four tiny single cabins with two baths, a deck lounge cabin, and a dining saloon. Such limitations were necessary to obtain 32 knots on 225′ length.

Many of the other owners were men who had made their money quickly and enjoyed spending it, not infrequently with an eye for personal glorification or maximum display. They were often entirely ignorant of yachting and could not or would not understand the limitations or options demanded in yacht design and construction. They could not understand why they should settle for a very costly yacht that could not go as fast as a simple horse. In many cases they were most unreasonable in other demands when considering a yacht. Clinton Crane, one of the most eminent engineers in yacht design, refers to his problems with W. B. Leeds in the design and construction of *Noma*. Leeds and Daniel Reid, a partner in the sale of the tin-plate trust to U.S. Steel Co., ordered twin steam yachts from Clinton Crane, 186′ LWL. Reid left the design to Clinton Crane, who supervised her construction. *Rheclair*, Daniel Reid's yacht, turned out to be a most successful vessel. W. B. Leeds, on the other hand, continually changed his mind. After the first design was completed he wanted a larger and faster yacht. He insisted on large fresh-water gravity tanks, which being high up reduced stability. He had special oversized porcelain bathtubs fitted, which, too, were high topside weight. He had his house decorator do the interior of his yacht in heavy, carved panelling. Then, having specified three foot width for the corridors; he went through them with a double pointed stick just three feet long. Everywhere the panelling was scratched it had to be carved down to size. Whenever the designer protested, Mr. Leeds would say, "How much will that extra bathtub reduce stability?" or "How much speed will that take off?" or "Well, can't you add some more power?" The yacht was lengthened, reboilered, and reengined, and eventually due to the engineering skills of Mr. Crane the designer, and of the yard, a suitable vessel resulted, one that put in 30 years of service. Other owners, too, had little knowledge or experience to appreciate the balance their desires demanded and what could be built. Furthermore, technically trained engineers with experience in yacht design were few in the early days, Capt. Nat Herreshoff being an outstanding exception. The American Society of Naval Architects started in only 1893, so either yachtsmen would go directly to a builder, who usually tried to improve on a vessel he had already built, or the owner's captain would try to have a vessel built according to his ideas, or the yachtsman would go to Britain where the standard of technical training was more advanced and where they had had greater experience in yacht design. Later on designers such as Charles Seabury and Clinton Crane were outstanding, and the craftsmanship in yards such as Herreshoff, Lawley, Marvel, Seabury (later Consolidated) was superb.

Even so, the great majority of yachts in the United States were used for commuting and short trips, and for a while faster and larger yachts were built. It is difficult to appreciate now the importance and the extent of water travel in those days. As recently as the 1930's that well-known body of water, Long Island Sound, connecting New York City with southern New England ports, enjoyed EACH WAY NIGHTLY to and from New York:

(a) A Fall River-Newport steamer; palatial craft over 400' long and carrying 1500 passengers overnight at prices as low as $3 (compared to over $11 for a seat in a railway coach today) in a two berth cabin. Deluxe dining facilities (in 1908) offered a whole boiled lobster for 75¢ and tenderloin steak for 60¢. A special boat train connected Fall River and Boston.

(b) A direct Boston boat, of comparable opulence.

(c) A New Bedford boat.

(d) Two competing Providence boats.

(e) A Norwich-New London boat.

(f) A Hartford boat.

Similiar nightly services accommodated Baltimore-Norfolk and Washington-Norfolk and many other ports especially out of and north of Boston.

The Fall River Line, probably the best known, operated for 90 years nightly, winter and summer, without electronic aids to navigation and for most years without radio, under some of the worst weather and traffic conditions imaginable, yet lost only one passenger out of more than two million carried. As early as 1857, their *Metropolis* made the 122 statute miles from Execution Rock to Point Judith in 6 hours, 2 minutes or 20.9 miles per hour. Now there are no passenger line services on the Sound. Yacht owners such as the Bordens would travel between their homes in New Jersey and their mills in Fall River; or H.H. Rogers would go back and forth to Fairhaven, Massachusetts. Others would savor the social delights of Newport or visit summer homes at Fisher's Island, Narragansett, Cape Cod, and other points eastward.

Some of these yachts, such as *Kanahwa*, *Corsair*, *Noma*, and *Hauoli*, were faster than the usual seagoing craft. Gradually it became evident that comfort and seaworthiness were incompatible with high speed, so a group of destroyer-like high-speed yachts evolved, among them the Bordens' later *Sovereigns*, Peter Rouss's four *Winchesters*, and William Zeig-

ler's *Gem*. These yachts carried their owners along the coast in comfort, if not in splendor. A story is told of Mr. Borden, returning to New York in *Little Sovereign*, being overhauled and passed by one of the *Winchesters*. Turning to his captain, he said "Don't stop at the Yacht Club landing, but continue on to Seabury's yard so I can order a faster yacht." The four-funnelled *Sovereign* was the result. Some of these yachts were turbine powered and some still retained the reciprocating engines. Some burned coal, others oil. Later on a smaller type of craft was developed exclusively for commuting use. Such craft as *Niagara IV*, *Navette*, and the Herreshoff Scouts had little or no sleeping accomodation for the owner, but simply a lounge, a bath for changing clothes, and a galley to provide morning breakfasts or afternoon tea served while travelling between home and New York City.

The effect of length on the speed (and of course power) of displacement craft is very great. Naturally V-bottom or stepped bottom plaining craft behave quite differently. As typical examples: British V or W class destroyers, 312' long, 1300 tons displacement, could make 33 knots on 27,000 horsepower. The British battlecruiser *Repulse*, built at the same time so with presumably the same knowledge of naval architecture, was 794' long, with 32,700 tons displacement (or 25 times that of the V or W craft). She would make the same speed (33 knots) on 120,000 brake horsepower (or only 4½ times the power of the destroyers.)

To show the enormous increase of power required at increased speed the following table may be of interest. The British A class destroyers of 1927 are used as an example.

SPEED VS HORSEPOWER—
"A" CLASS DESTROYER OF 1927

Horsepower	Speed in knots
1000	11.9
2000	14.8
3500	17.0
5000	18.6
10000	22.8
20000	26.8
34000	31.5

Thus, to increase such vessels' speed 5.9 knots in the 15 knot range required 2500 horsepower and it took over 15,000 horsepower to increase the same speed at the 29 knot level.

To return to American steam yachts, most of the early ones were for use in protected waters, so watertube boilers, higher pressures, and wooden hulls (lighter than the heavy iron and steel ones built in Britain, where metal construction was more advanced than in the United States) were in common use in the United States. Fast steam launches were widely used. Some of these were quite notable craft. For example, *Ellide*, designed by that most capable engineer C. D. Mosher and built of wood by S. Ayer of Nyack, New York, was 81′ LOA by 8′ beam and weighed 13 tons. She made 40 statute miles per hour (34.2 knots) on trials. But as far as cruising was concerned, voyages to the now popular West Indies or elsewhere were few and far between, since time was an element of utmost concern. Only a few owners could make such cruises. Even J. Pierpont Morgan would travel to Europe and back on liners of the White Star Line, a prominent part of the International Mercantile Marine that Mr. Morgan had been instrumental in founding. He would send *Corsair* to Europe to meet him, and when he went to Rome, Paris, or London before returning, *Corsair* would go back and make it a point of pride to go down to the Narrows entrance of New York harbor to greet the owner as he approached on the White Star liner. Some of the Vanderbilt family, or the Astors, James Gordon Bennett, Henry Walters, George F. Baker, Jr., and Arthur Curtiss James would make extensive cruises, but these were in the minority. These owners had fine seagoing craft.

Life on board the larger yachts in the United States was, at times, somewhat more lively than on British ones. First, yachts could be moored right in New York City, where facilities for gaiety were present, whereas English yachts could not approach London so easily. Secondly, several owners enjoyed their newly acquired wealth in a rather strenuous manner. One yacht was famous (or infamous, depending on the point of view) for the frequent *danse du ventre* performances given on her afterdeck. Another had a luxurious owner's cabin complete with an electric console control board. Push one button, and soft music was heard. Push another and a small bar opened into view. Push a third, and the wall beside the owner's bed rolled away to find the guest of the evening, having retired to the assumed sanctity of her private cabin, revealed in a bed beside that of the owner. Sherman Hoyt once told of an incident while waiting to go ashore from a yacht to church. The Sunday calm of Newport was rent by a scream from an adjacent yacht. This was quickly followed by the appearance on deck of a curvaceous blond in a filmy nightgown, screaming "You won't ------- me again, you S.O.B.!" as she plunged overboard. There was more screaming when she realized she couldn't swim! As the waiting launch made a very public rescue in which the nightgown kept slipping off the body of the rescued, a huge bearded man, completely nude, came on deck, admonishing the launch crew to "Let the double-crossing bitch drown!"

Possibly the opposite extreme in behavior occurred in England. In the 1880's a Bayard Brown chartered a yacht. Enchanted with yachting, he bought the first *Lady Torfrida* from Sir William Pearce, her builder and owner. The yacht was staffed with a complete crew and provisioned and fuelled for a cruise. She lay at anchor near Brightlingsea on Britain's east coast, without moving for over two years. Whatever others thought about this lack of movement is not known, but Mr. Brown enjoyed his life aboard so much that he sold her and bought the second and larger *Lady Torfrida*, changing her name to *Valfreyia*. There the new yacht lay at anchor, month after month, year after year, without moving, until World War I started. The British Admiralty, desperate for craft of any kind, inspected her, but had to reject her for neglect of maintenance. They forced her, however, to vacate her mooring place, so she went upriver for the duration of the war. There she lay with her owner still aboard. The crew, accustomed to board her daily and return to home each evening, went into war service. After the war *Valfreyia* was almost in sinking condition. She was docked for rebuilding. Mr. Brown enjoyed life in the drydock, even though at times, with the plating removed, he had nothing but a tarpaulin between his stateroom and the elements. For over a year she remained, at her owner's expense, in the dock. Eventually she returned to her old anchorage off Brightlingsea until 1927, when after 38 years of ownership and living aboard, Mr. Brown died.

Of the serious owners, George F. Baker, Jr., a banker, was a good example. He had owned one *Viking* of limited cruising range for several years, before he had a new *Viking* built in 19 months by Newport News in 1929. She was a comfortable, long-ranged, seaworthy vessel with turbo-electric drive. For the next eight years she was almost continuously cruising, being laid up six weeks or so each January or February in New London for maintenance. Her owner, a devoted fisherman, would follow the fish to Maine, Georges Bank, Nova Scotia, the St. Lawrence in summer, and go to the West Indies, Galapagos, and the west coast of South America in the northern winters, often going to the Mediterranean in spring or fall. In 1937 she started on a round-the-world cruise with just enough fuel capacity to go on one engine economically from Panama to Tahiti. There she refuelled 76,000 gallons from nearly 1500 drums by hand! On the way to Australia Mr. Baker became ill, so *Viking* diverted to Honolulu where her owner died. Capt. Edwin Thompson of Deer Isle, Maine was with Mr. Baker for over 30 years. *Viking* usually had a crew of 47; captain, three mates, a radioman, three quartermasters, and 15 hands. The chief engineer had three assistants, an electrician, three oilers, three firemen and three wipers. The chief steward had an assistant, two bedroom stewards, two cooks, and four messboys.

Arthur Curtiss James was owner of the brig and the bark-rigged *Aloha*. He was a dedicated cruising man. In the brig *Aloha* he cruised to the Mediterranean and Adriatic in 1900, to the West Indies in 1902, to Iceland, Faroes, Norway, and England in 1903, to Scotland in 1905, to England in 1906, 1907 (via Newfoundland). On the bark *Aloha* he went again to England and Scotland on her first voyage in 1910, to Panama and to Ireland the next year, to Egypt and the Near East in 1912–13. After World War I he went around the world in 1921–22, to the Mediterranean and Venice in 1925, to England, the Baltic, and Holland in 1927, and to the Mediterranean again in 1930. On such a voyage *Aloha* had a crew of captain, two mates, carpenter, boatswain, radioman, and 16 hands. She carried in the engine room a chief and two assistant engineers, two oilers, and two firemen, while the stewards department comprised nine including a stewardess.

One great trouble encountered by such inveterate cruising owners was to find people of congenial dispositions who had the available time to make these extended cruises. J. Pierpont Morgan once said, "Have you got one or two men whom you are fond of, that you can depend on always to go off yachting with you? Because if you haven't, don't buy a yacht, as it will be the loneliest place in the world for you."

Most officers of American yachts came from Maine or other coastal ports, though a few were ex-square rigger seamen or came from the merchant marine. Places like Deer Isle, Maine supplied many of them. Its youngsters grew up on the water and, when old enough, would ship with a relative or neighbor on a yacht. Thus a steady stream of able men came from Deer Isle, first as yacht hands, then rising to mates and captains. Many would spend their entire career with one owner or his family. Gradually Norwegians and other Scandinavians or men from the Baltic Sea would grow from positions as hands to become officers. A few such as Captain Porter of the *Corsair* came from the merchant marine as in those days pay was better on yachts and there was greater chance for advancement. Some others such as Capt. Edward Geer of *Kanahwa*, came from, and in his case went back to, the Fall River Line, or other coasting services. Engineers, too, came from Maine and other ports. Few, if any, came out of shipyards or engine shops. Chiefs would prefer to take on intelligent but completely unskilled youngsters and train them up to their standards than to take on men who had had some experience. As the supply of local boys became smaller, more and more Scandinavians (especially Norwegians) and Baltics, with occasional Germans or Hollanders, became the principal source of crews. Sometimes whole villages in Norway would be employed on American yachts.

In the 1880's and 1890's captains would get around $150–$200 per month as would chief engineers. Mates and assistant engineers got $45–$100, hands and firemen made about $30, chief stewards earned $60–$100, while a good cook's wage was a secret between him and the owner. On United States yachts all hands were fed by the yacht. This is a far cry from present rates of $700–$1000 or over for a captain, $500–$1000 for a chief engineer, $600–$800 for chief stewards, and $200 for hands and firemen.

After World War I there was a noticeable decrease in new construction of all kinds, and particularly in large yachts powered by steam. In the United States, *Lyndonia* was built in 1920, at considerable expense because materials used in her construction had been purchased by her builder at war-inflated prices. *Alert* was another. *Delphine*, built on the Great Lakes, was another. In Britain, *Cutty Sark* was devised by Yarrow from materials left over from cancelled destroyer construction. *Restless* and *Thalassa* were among the steamers built in Britain soon after the war. Sir Walter Guinness, later Lord Moyne, had conversions made of cross-channel steamers. No one seemed interested in converting any of the fast *Gray* class of steam turbine powered fast gunboats of World War II. Toward the latter part of the 1920's the boom market gave a spurt of new construction of larger and larger yachts, but these, with a few notable exceptions such as *Corsair*, *Viking*, and *Nahlin*, were all diesel powered. Construction of several of these yachts extended into the early 1930's, after the depression had begun, as they had been contracted for, or were under construction when the crash occurred. But already that relentless and most influential of all yacht designers, the Internal Revenue Service, was making its policies felt. The diesels occupied smaller space; did not have many auxiliaries such as boilers, condensers, and numerous feed and circulating pumps; provided better utilization of interior layouts. Lighter materials permitted higher superstructures. All this meant that nearly the same accomodations for owner and guests were possible on much smaller vessels. In recent years still smaller yachts have resulted from rapidly increasing costs, as well as from these design improvements. In 1963 a steel power yacht 105' LOA (about 150 TYM) was built in the Netherlands, where costs are considerably lower than in the United States, for an estimated cost of $700,000, nearly three times the reputed cost of Jay Gould's 248' *Atalanta* in 1883, eighty years before.

Now in the sixties, several yachts of 120–140' LOA are being built but all are diesel powered. Alas, the leisured class of the steam yacht era has disappeared. Large yachts are now used by wealthy but busy men, and whole winters in the Mediterranean or Caribbean or on world cruises are a thing of the past. People fly to the cruising grounds and join the yachts there, and after their holidays, return by air. Most of these yachts, too, are now owned for tax reasons by companies. They are used by the executives of the owning company for entertaining customers or for other business reasons that can be written off as non-taxable expenses. Other yachts owned by companies are available for charters as a business venture. Again for tax reasons, many also are registered in and fly the flag of countries "of convenience" such as Panama, Liberia, Honduras.

POWER PLANTS

Throughout the era, from the introduction of the screw propeller, most steam yachts were powered by triple expansion engines, with coal-fired Scotch boilers. Of course there were many exceptions. Early yachts, such as *North Star*, or the early *Victoria and Albert, Osborne*, or the first *Hohenzollern*, were paddle steamers. Others, later, had single expansion condensing, compound, and in a few cases quadruple expansion engines. Later some of the express type of post-World War I yachts were turbine powered, at first direct drive, later geared or turbo-electric. A short description of each will illustrate the different types.

BOILERS

The Scotch boiler was introduced in the 1850's–1860's in Britain. Previous to its introduction the "box" and other flue and fire-tube boilers had been used. It was, and is, a fire-tube (against a water-tube) boiler and is basically the same as a railroad locomotive boiler, without the limitations of height and width imposed on locomotives. It is a large cylindrical drum, lying on its side, filled with water. At one end is a firebox. A number of tubes carry the hot gases from the firebox, through the water in the drum, where they emerge into a smoke stack or funnel. The marine Scotch boiler is proportionally shorter than the locomotive one, but bigger in diameter. Scotch boilers were eventually good to around 180 pounds per square inch pressure, but had to be heated up and cooled down slowly to avoid damage by expansion or contraction of the large shell. From cold, several hours were necessary to raise steam to its working pressure. The bridge had to advise the boiler room well in advance before shutting down the engines so fires could be banked. As a result, steam was kept up in Scotch boilers, with fires at least banked, during quite long periods when not under way. This practice was more suitable to British yachts, which were normally under way for longer periods than were American yachts, more often used for commuting runs or on weekends. Hence, British yachts retained

Scotch boilers long after most American ones had gone to water-tube boilers. Scotch boilers also suffered by their heavy weight for the steam generated, by the limitations in length of the boiler, and by their general inefficiency in the amount of steam generated for the fuel consumed.

Water-tube boilers started to come into use on yachts in the 1860's and 1870's even though they were known of in the early 1800's. Herreshoff, by training a steam engineer and initially a steam engine designer, built a coil-type water-tube boiler in 1873. Most of his designs thereafter had water-tube boilers. Drum boilers were initially the most common of the water-tube designs. By means of baffles, the hot gases could reach more than one row of the many small tubes of water. The gases, thus used more intensively, resulted in the need for less water in the boiler, for lighter weight and for considerably greater economy. Boiler walls became water cooled, and superheaters could be installed. The two-drum design, with a steam drum over a water drum connected by straight water tubes, was an improvement. In 1889 Sir Alfred Yarrow patented the now widely used three-drum boiler, with two water drums at both lower corners of the boiler connected in the form of an inverted V by many small water tubes to a single steam drum above. A firebox was located inside the inverted V. At present this is probably the most popular express water-tube boiler, though of course there are many other designs and improvements. In water-tube boilers steam could be raised rapidly as there was much less water in the boiler.

Experiments are still under way with flash-type high-pressure boilers having automatic feed, and water and fuel controls. These boilers do not have the three-drum type arrangement but have intricately arranged coils. Such boilers can reach 1500 pounds pressure from cold in less than one minute, providing just the amount of steam that is required at the moment from zero to full demand in a matter of a few seconds, so little is the amount of water and steam in the system. Such boilers are made of special materials such as Nitralloy, so they are costly to make and maintain. The New Haven Railroad operated a railcar unit for over a year with a Besler flash steam plant. This unit is described later under "Engines." It had its boiler in the baggage compartment and its engine in one of the trucks. Considering it was an experimental unit installed in a railway car already in existence, it operated most satisfactorily, and with proper development could have been made into a successful modern steam plant.

ENGINES

The *North Star* and some other early yachts were paddle wheelers. *North Star* had two cylinders 60″ in diameter with a stroke of 120″ operating her paddles via walking beams, a common feature on American steamers up to the early 1900's. On screw steamers, single-stage engines were used at first, but the alternate cooling and heating of the cylinder walls made for unsatisfactory operation. This, together with the early use of sea water in boilers, the frequent need to "blow" brine and salt from the boilers, the non-condensing feature of many units (as in railroad locomotives or some harbor tugs a few years ago), or condensing by mixing exhaust steam with sea water, resulted in quite inefficient power generation. Soon surface condensers (as in condensers or radiators today, where the coolant and condensate are always separated) and compounding of the steam engines were developed with considerable improvement in maintenance and economy. Fortunately most steam yachts were spared these early difficulties. Compound engines, developed in the 1860's, were ones in which steam from the boiler was admitted into one cylinder, which in turn exhausted the steam, now at a lower pressure, into a second cylinder of larger bore. The exhaust from this low-pressure cylinder, at a still lower pressure and temperature, went into the condcnser. Thus more effective use was made of the available steam, and by maintaining each cylinder at a more constant temperature, less wear resulted.

Once compounding proved to be more economical, a triple expansion engine with a third stage was the logical outcome, and it came into use about 1870. A further stage, a quadruple expansion engine, was tried, but the limitations on steam pressure in Scotch boilers and the extra complication of another stage did not overcome the simplicity of the triple expansion engine, so few quads were built. Most reciprocating-engined yachts will be found to have triple expansion engines. For each size of cylinders in decreasing steam pressures, a cylinder of larger bore, commensurate with the entering steam pressure, was required. Frequently, the lowest pressure stage, instead of employing a single, heavy, large-diameter

cylinder assembly would use two small low-pressure cylinders, which between them could replace the single large-diameter one. These smaller piston assemblies were easier to balance and provided a more even driving force.

Until quite recently the valves on steam engines were slide valves, as on nearly all railroad locomotive engines, and were driven by eccentrics on the main crankshaft. N. G. Herreshoff, originally a designer for the Corliss Steam Engine Co., started to design engines for craft built by his blind brother John B. until he went into partnership in 1878. From then on he designed and supervised the construction of both sail and steam craft as well as the engines and boilers. He was devoted to light weight and some of his engines are still beautiful because of their light yet rigid construction. His five-cylinder quadruple engines built for *Ballymena, Say When, Vamoose,* and USS *Cushing* were notable for their steel forgings and rod construction instead of heavy iron castings used by other builders. To shorten the engines, thus permitting more rigid crankshafts, Herreshoff moved all valve gear drives to a separate camshaft located beside and parallel to the crankshaft, permitting the cylinders to be close together instead of separated by valves and drives. Another feature of his was to build "steeple" engines with one or more (usually the low-pressure) cylinders located above the others, thus shortening (and stiffening) the engine. He was probably the first to build centrifugally cast, hollow steel crankshafts that were lighter and stiffer than those machined from normal forgings. Ford revolutionized the engine world when they introduced similar crankshafts on the first Ford V-8's, nearly 30 years later. Herreshoff also was one of the first to enclose the crankcase on steam engines, permitting splash lubrication, as is done now on all automotive engines. He experimented with poppet valves in several engines, as did some railroads toward the end of the steam locomotive era.

Some experiments have been made in recent years on very high pressure, completely automatic small steam engines. A Besler installation of 150 horsepower at 1200 RPM and weighing, complete with engine (180 pounds) boiler, feed water, condenser, pumps, etc., 665 pounds actually flew in a small open-cockpit Travelair biplane. The New Haven railcar referred to above under "Boilers" had the Besler boiler installed in the baggage compartment of an ordinary railcar. The engine was built into one of the trucks or bogies. This unit ran successfully for over a year, but maintenance costs were rather high. The railroad shops were not familiar with the close limits, new materials, or high pressures of that design. One man in particular, in the engineering department, sponsored this experiment, but when he left, the project died, the power plant was removed, and the car reverted to normal service. Furthermore diesels were coming into use on railroads about that time. The potential of diesel drive appeared brighter, so available engineering talent could not be diverted from diesel to a highly experimental high-pressure steam design that would require considerable time and effort to prove itself in service use.

McCulloch, makers of, among other things, small gasoline engines for lawn mowers and other uses, did considerable development work on steam powered automotive plants. Using the latest (1950's) data available to them, they produced a boiler for automotive use, 18″ in diameter by 27″ long, weighing 188 pounds, that released 1.2 million BTU per hour at 2000 pounds pressure and 900 F temperature. This steam powered a three-cylinder double-acting compound engine $1\frac{3}{4}″ \times 3\frac{3}{4}″/3\frac{1}{2}″$ that produced 120 horsepower and weighed 285 pounds. The total weight of the whole installation including feed water and lubricating oil was 953 pounds. It was installed and ran most successfully in an automobile called "Paxton." Before attempting any form of production, McCulloch and his associates studied the engineering talent that would be necessary to develop such an automobile to the point of commercial production, as well as the costs that would be required. They found that the necessary expenditure of engineers would too seriously handicap the development and production of other products on which their livelihood depended. They could not foresee sufficient availability of experimental time or funds, in the near future, to develop such an automobile to a production level. So, reluctantly, they had to give up the whole project, having proven, to their satisfaction, its practical potential. An interesting paper on this project was published in the SAE Journal in 1962.

TURBINES

The first successful marine turbine was developed in England by Charles Parsons. He dramatically demonstrated turbine power in *Turbinia* at the Royal Naval Review in 1897. Three direct drive turbines, each of a different steam pressure stage and each driving a separate propeller shaft, developed a total of 2000 horsepower. Each shaft had three propellers to absorb the power and avoid cavitation. *Turbinia* tore through the assembled fleet, which included representatives of major navies of the world, at 35 knots giving a most conclusive demonstration of turbine power. A coastal steamer, *King Edward*, was the first large ship installation of turbines. The 20,000 ton Cunarder *Carmania* came soon after. Her performance was so satisfactory that the new, huge (for then), fast Cunarders *Mauretania* and *Lusitania*

were turbine powered. In spite of these demonstrations, yachts, except for a few express designs, did not take to turbines to any great extent. The *Tarantula* of 1902, an express type, and *Emerald* were the first turbine powered yachts. The expense, the poor maneuvering qualities of turbines (especially direct drive) compared to the "up-and-down" reciprocating engines, and above all the lack of familiarity of turbines by yacht engineers mitigated against them. Some express yachts, especially in the United States, and after World War I, a few turbo-electric craft, were about the only turbine powered yachts. The first turbine yacht in the United States was probably *Revolution* of 1902, designed by C.L. Seabury with Curtis turbines provided by their builder and her owner, G.C. Curtis.

Turbines, to be efficient, must operate at relatively high revolutions. Direct drive turbines turn too fast for any reasonable propeller efficiency. Yet to slow them down is most inefficient for turbine performance. This is especially noticeable at cruising or low speeds. Reduction gears solve the problem but are costly and noisy, with a high-pitched gear whine. They still do not improve the maneuverability of vessels. Geared turbines are more acceptable in fast passenger vessels and large tankers where maneuvering is infrequent and is aided by tugs.

Turbo-electric drive solves the maneuvering problem and is quiet. It is however, costly, more complicated, a bit heavier, and slightly less economical than geared turbines. *Corsair* (4th) and *Viking* are good examples of turbo-electric yachts.

The smoothness and silence of steam drive were among the more attractive features, especially before the silencing and balancing of diesels was improved. They were still influential factors even though better diesels became available. However, people would forget the space required for steam plants; the filth of frequent coaling; the cinders (or on oil burners, the soot) from the funnels of steam yachts; the need (particularly in small yachts) to have, at all times under way, at least one engineer-cum-fireman to handle the controls and to maintain the boiler working properly; and above all the far greater economy in fuel consumption of a diesel engine. On quite large diesel yachts direct bridge control is installed.

Daniel Cox of Cox & Stevens pointed out that a steam powered equivalent of the 163′ diesel yacht *Ohio* with the same speed of 12 knots and a 10,000 mile range would have 10% less space available for accommodation, would need a further four men, and fuel would cost three times as much while under way and nearly 15 times as much when still. Actually the accommodation in a 100′ steam yacht can now be found in a 65′ diesel yacht.

Steam boilers, especially Scotch boilers, required

ample room in front for the firing and drawing of boiler tubes, as well as insulation space all around the boiler to prevent the transmission of heat. Even if oil fuel is used, space in front is needed to handle burners and to draw tubes. The steam engine (except possibly for "steeple" types) was larger than a diesel of equal power. Space had to be provided for bulky condensers, air pumps, circulating pumps, feed pumps, forced draft blowers, etc. Coal bunkers took up a great deal of space as they had to be adjacent to the furnaces. Space was needed for hot ashes. Bulky condensers would constantly leak, admitting sea water to the feed water resulting in boiler scale. Of course, toward the end of the steam yacht era, oil fuel improved the space available over coal burners. Fuel could be in bottoms or elsewhere. No space was needed for ash handling, refueling was clean, and the need for constant fire-room work was reduced or eliminated. With the experimental high-pressure flash systems, if cost were no object, quite suitable automated, bridge-controlled steam power plants could be developed. But with any reciprocating steam engine, the fuel costs are far higher than with a diesel. On large vessels geared turbines are often cheaper initially and frequently cost less to maintain than diesels, while fuel consumption approaches any but the most efficient diesels. In tankers in particular, the fore-and-aft space required by a turbine drive is often less than a diesel, especially when the boiler is mounted above the engine room. However, these advantages apply to larger vessels of 20,000 tons or more.

The only possibility of development of steam power suitable for yachts and their manufacture at a reasonable cost is a campaign against smog, especially in Los Angeles and other major cities, reaching a level of public demand for vehicles that do not pollute the air as do gasoline or diesel powered automotive vehicles, which are now the major offenders. Already there are severe limits on exhaust emissions, and such laws will undoubtedly become more strict in the near future. Major motor car manufacturers have several steam powered cars in the research stage. Maybe something will result. If so, the problem with rapid acceleration and deceleration now plaguing steam engine development in motor cars, together with the limitations imposed by motor

car dimensions, will not be a problem when such units are adapted to marine uses.

With the exception of such legal restrictions on internal combustion engines that may be imposed, we feel that the diesel is here to stay in yachts and a renaissance of steam has slim hopes.

The only possible competitor to the diesel that may be on the horizon is the gas turbine, either direct combustion or fed by a free-piston diesel. Gas turbines are, of course, widely used in aircraft, usually now as pure jets. The Union Pacific Railroad in the United States has a number of gas turbine locomotives and is apparently pleased with them. Recently several yacht-sized vessels, mainly high-speed naval craft, are being fitted with gas turbines, usually Bristol Proteus or Canadian Pratt & Whitney PT6. The gas turbine suffers from the handicaps of penetrating noise and odor, high initial cost, and at present, high fuel consumption, nearly twice as high as a diesel. Its light weight, small dimensions, and lack of reciprocating parts are in its favor. Improvements should occur in time to reduce some of the disadvantages.

The free-piston version has an opposed piston diesel as the gas generator instead of direct combustion. Not being connected to crankshafts, the opposed pistons float and are cushioned on the downstroke by large air-compressing pistons. The gases exhausted from this engine are fed into a gas turbine. Thus the combustion, being on a diesel cycle, where it about equals the normal diesel, is far below that of the direct consumption gas turbine. Its disadvantages are the cost of two separate propulsion systems, and the greater space it occupies. The Pescara and other free-piston units were installed in several vessels in the 1950's, but the development does not seem to have progressed as projected.

Nuclear power, which is basically a steam turbine with a highly efficient boiler, is out for yachts until some 100% safe insulation against uranium radiation activity is developed that is only a fraction of the weight and bulk required now. When that is achieved, there will still be the factor of high initial cost. Nuclear power allows infinitesimal fuel consumption permitting long range, and, not requiring oxygen in air for combustion, it can be completely sealed as in a submerged submarine.

INDIVIDUAL STEAM YACHTS

Over one hundred typical steam yachts are briefly described with their principal specifications, photographs, and in many cases drawings by R. R. Moore. They are listed in order of the year in which they were built or converted to yachts, and by their first name as a yacht. The list covers representatives of various types of yachts and does not attempt to cover all, or those of one type. An omission of a yacht does not denote that it is in any way inferior to one listed. Possibly data or a photograph is missing. Omitted entirely are those under 75′ LOA, as well as open launches. I realize full well that I will receive numerous objections to this selection, that such and such was better than one shown, or that my grandfather's yacht *Blank* was flagship of an important club and should be shown.

The data, dimensions, specifications, and ownership are as close as can be found at the present time. There is a great deal of unavoidable confusion. The same name appears on more than one yacht. For example, Fairfield built three *Lady Torfridas*, all for Sir William Pearce. The first at 623 Thames measurement, built in 1883, later became *Tamara*. The second, of 735 Thames tonnage and built in 1888, became *Valfreyia* and *Star of India*. The third, of 593 Thames tonnage and built in 1890, remained *Lady Torfrida*. There were three *Venetias*, two by the same designers, Cox & King, of nearly the same size. One, of 687 Thames tonnage and built in 1903, was mostly owned in North America and always called *Venetia*. The other, of 568 Thames tonnage, built in 1905, was owned in the United Kingdom (until sold to commercial interests), having had several names. The third *Venetia* (1893) became the *North Star*. Two other yachts each bore both the names *Semiramis* and *Margarita* during their lives. Dimensions varied according to the source. Sometimes a registered length was shown (especially in the older British Lloyd's), sometimes length over all. Sometimes, the overall length as reported included the bowsprit on clipper-bowed yachts for the owners' greater satisfaction. Tonnages, Yacht Club lists, magazine descriptions, builders' figures often dif-

fered from yacht registers. Sometimes the British and American Lloyd's showed differences for the same yacht or varied even in different editions of the same Lloyd's.

There are various tonnages used for reporting. In the United Kingdom, Thames Yacht Measurement (TYM) tonnage was, and is still, used as the principal yardstick for the size of yachts. This measurement:

$$(L - B) \times B \times \frac{B}{2} \div 94$$ was adopted by the Yacht

Racing Association in England in 1879 as a handicapping formula for sailing yachts. It was found that in many yachts of that era the sum of the overhangs about equalled the beam. To obtain an opproximation of the waterline length, which was difficult to measure, on a yacht afloat, a defined, easily measured length-minus-beam gave a near enough approximation. Furthermore, in yachts of that period it was noticed that the depth was around half the beam, so the B/2, which could be measured afloat, was used to symbolize depth. It can be seen that beam plays a most important factor in Thames measurement, yet this formula, now 90 years old, is still in popular use in the United Kingdom. Builders still quote prices on Thames tonnage whether for keel sailboats or power boats or yachts such as steam yachts. The Thames tonnage is usually a bit greater than the gross tonnage.

Gross tonnage and its related net tonnage are the internationally accepted measurements for vessels. Both are purely volumetric measurements having nothing to do with tons as the weight of a vessel. These tonnages are carefully defined, but the definitions vary among countries. Basically, gross tonnage is the enclosed volume of a vessel in which 100 cubic feet equals one ton. Net tonnage, on which harbor, canal, pilot, and other fees are based, is gross tonnage minus all nonrevenue producing space (excluding fuel, water, galley, crew, navigational, and machinery spaces but including cargo, and passenger enclosed spaces). It is evident that these can be altered to some extent. The *SS Leviathan* came out as the

25

54,000 gross tons *Vaterland*. Her near, but slightly longer, sister *Hindenberg* (which became *Majestic*) was 56,000 gross tons. To make the *Leviathan* the "World's Largest Ship," windows on the covered passenger decks were closed, and together with other tricks, her tonnage was increased to 59,000 gross tons. Some years later when newer and faster vessels were on the Atlantic, and operational costs became a more important factor than advertised size, the *Leviathan* was "remeasured" and her tonnage dropped to 49,000 tons. While on the subject of tonnage, two other tonnages not related to yachts might be mentioned. Both are "weight" tonnages. Displacement, the actual weight of a vessel in long tons (2240 pounds), is used mainly for naval vessels. Bulk cargo vessels, particularly oil or grain carriers, are often referred to by their "deadweight" tonnage or the actual weight, also in long tons (2240 pounds), of the cargo they can carry. Some new tankers can now transport cargo weighing five times the actual weight of the *Queen Mary*.

The appearance of yachts often changes during their lifetime. Both *Cyprus* and *Noma* were changed from one to two funnels. Additional deckhouses were fitted. As time went on, the helmsman was given greater protection, until wheelhouses and enclosed bridges were installed. Yards and sails were removed. Thus a photograph or drawing of a yacht could easily differ from another taken at a different stage of her life. Those yachts that were in war service, particularly World War II, were often drastically altered to the extent of being unidentifiable. Bowsprits were removed, ports in the hull were plated over, different masts replaced former ones and were so located to be suitable for radar installations and signal hoists. New deckhouses or more adaptable bridges were fitted. A good example of such changes is that of USS *Mayflower* in her World War II Coast Guard Service.

Thus, in spite of all possible care, there will be cases of confusion, varying dimensions, etc. All that can be done is to try to eliminate known inaccuracies and avoid misunderstandings as far as possible.

It is difficult to obtain data, information, anecdotes, etc., on steam yachts because little has been recorded in print and most people familiar with them have passed on. The publication of one book may release many memories. I would greatly appreciate any scrap of information on these or any other cruising steam yachts that any reader may have, their activities, performances, cruises, who the owners were, what they did, anecdotes about them and the vessels' captains, engineers, and stewards. I would welcome any photographs clear enough to permit making a good copy so that the original can be returned. It is only through such interest on the part of readers that many desirable records come to light. Such contributions can be sent to me care of the publisher: John deGraff, 34 Oak Ave, Tuckahoe, N.Y. 10707.

TABLE OF INDIVIDUAL YACHTS

27

NORTH STAR ~ 1853

DESIGNER: *Jeremiah Simonson*
BUILT: *1853* BY *Jeremiah Simonson,*
               Greenport, L.I.
MATERIAL: *Wood*   RIG: *Paddle Schooner*

LOA	LWL	BEAM	DRAFT in feet
270		36	

GROSS TON	NET TON	TYM	DISP
1876			

POWER: BOILER   ENGINE
        Paddle—2 Beam Engines, 60/120

BHP (TOTAL)	SPEED (KNOTS)
	14.5

OWNERS:
Comdre. Cornelius Vanderbilt 1853–1854
   Commercial service in companies owned by
   Vanderbilt

North Star was probably the first steam yacht in the United States. That she was converted to commercial service after her famous cruise has caused some people to say that she was not a yacht. According to descriptions at the time, she was built and luxuriously fitted out solely as a yacht. She was somewhat unique in having two walking beams. Commodore Cornelius Vanderbilt was a growing ship owner who later organized and headed the New York Central Railroad system. He had *North Star* built for a cruise to Europe for himself and his large family as well as a doctor and clergyman and their wives. Reverend Choules had been to Europe a short time before and had published a description of his travels, so he was to be the chronicler of this cruise.

North Star sailed from New York on May 20, 1853. Her captain, Asa Eldridge, was a well-known North Atlantic packet ship master. Mrs. Eldridge was a guest on the cruise. (The following year Captain Eldridge commanded the new clipper *Red Jacket* on her initial and record transatlantic trip. He was later lost as master of the new Collins Line steamer, *Pacific*, which disappeared without a trace, but is believed to have hit an iceberg.) Many of the deck hands were young men of good families taking the opportunity of such a cruise. The Steward of the Racquet Club was aboard as purser, and one of the Cunard Line's best stewards acted as such on *North Star*. Trouble occurred with the experienced firemen, who struck before leaving and had to be replaced with a green group. Backing from the slip on departure, *North Star* grounded. She was docked in the nearby Navy Yard to insure that there was no damage.

North Star's voyage across was uneventful and comfortable. She averaged a little over 300 miles per day and picked up her pilot off the Isle of Wight 10 days, 8 hours, 40 minutes after dropping the Sandy Hook

pilot. The local pilot promptly put her aground near the Needles, but she got off without damage on the rising tide.

She visited the following ports during her "Grand Tour:" New York, Southampton, Copenhagen, Cronstadt (Russia), Le Havre, Gibraltar, Málaga, Livorno, Civitavecchia, Naples, Malta, Constantinople (now Istanbul), Gibraltar, Madeira, New York.

North Star was under way 58 days out of the 126 days of the voyage. Upon her return on September 23, 1853, she had averaged 259 miles per day while under way. Considering the time and the state of development of the steam engine, *North Star*'s cruise was a momentous feat. It demonstrated dramatically the growth and power of the new United States (and of course of Commodore Vanderbilt) as nothing else could. In each port elaborate visits, dinners, etc., were arranged and such cities as London, St. Petersburg (now Leningrad), Paris, Florence, and Rome were visited by the Commodore and his guests. The chronicler, Reverend Choules, impressed though he surely was, was probably correct in saying that the voyage was under such circumstances of splendor and enjoyment that he doubted if such could be undertaken again.

Soon afterward, Commodore Vanderbilt had *North Star* converted to commercial passenger service running between New York and Honduras (for California-bound passengers who crossed to the Pacific there). Later she was under charter to the Navy during the Civil War. She nearly foundered in a storm in 1865. She was finally taken to New London, Connecticut, where she was broken up about 1866.

Reverend Choules' book was widely distributed, so the fame of the first American steam yacht, so large and magnificent, has remained to this day. Copies of that book can still be found over 100 years after publication.

~

Although *VICTORIA and ALBERT* (2nd) cruised twice to Madeira and once to Trieste, she was used, especially after the death of the Prince Consort, mainly in British waters. She did make occasional short trips to Norway and to the Baltic. In 1863 she brought Princess Alexandra to England for her marriage to the then Prince of Wales, later King Edward VII.

Queen Victoria loved this yacht, and spent considerable time aboard. As she became older and more lonely, the Queen became more and more attached to familiar objects such as the yacht's furnishings, so many of which brought memories to her. It was a

moment of sadness when she was finally convinced that its days were reaching their end after over 40 years of service. She accepted the need for a new yacht, but wanted it to be as much like the old one and to have as many of the familiar furnishings as possible installed in the new *VICTORIA and ALBERT* (3rd). Queen Victoria died before the new vessel was commisioned, so this vessel spanned the major part of the Victorian era from the first *VICTORIA and ALBERT*, which became the first *OSBORNE* when this yacht was built, until she was replaced by the third *VICTORIA and ALBERT* in 1901. She was broken up in 1904.

VICTORIA AND ALBERT (2nd) ~ 1855

DESIGNER: *O. Lang*

BUILT: *1855* BY *Pembroke Dockyard*

MATERIAL: *Wood*   RIG: *Paddle Schooner*

OWNERS:
British Navy as Royal Yacht

LOA	LWL	BEAM	DRAFT in feet
300 LBP		40.3	16.3

GROSS TON	NET TON	TYM	DISP
		2243	2470

POWER: BOILER   ENGINE
   Scotch   *Paddle*

BHP (TOTAL)	SPEED (KNOTS)
2980 IHP	15.4

Mahroussa is not only one of the largest steam yachts ever built, but it is certainly the oldest still in existence and in service. She was built of iron over 100 years ago. From an ancient paddle steamer, she was transformed in 1905 to a modern, triple screw, turbine powered vessel. She had a thorough facelift-ing in Italy around her 85th birthday. Not too well known world wide she spent most of her life cruising in the eastern Mediterranean as the yacht for the rulers of Egypt through King Farouk. She was still in commission as a school ship in 1968.

MAHROUSSA ~ 1865

Other Names:
EL HORRIA

DESIGNER: *O. Lang*
BUILT: *1865* BY *Samauda Bros., Poplar*
MATERIAL: *Iron*   RIG: *Triple Screw Schooner*

LOA	LWL	BEAM	DRAFT in feet
°478	421.5	42.6	17.5

GROSS TON	NET TON	TYM	DISP
3762	1568	3658	3140

POWER: BOILER   ENGINE
     6 Scotch   *Paddle—2 Osc 100/96*
                      3 Parsons Turbines in 1905

BHP (TOTAL)	SPEED (KNOTS)
1600	11
6500	15

OWNERS:
Egyptian Government as Royal Yacht and in 1951
   as school ship

° *Lengthened 40' in 1872 and 16.5' in 1905 Final length shown.*

33

Due to her comparatively shallow draft *Osborne* could dock at the pier at Osborne House, Isle of Wight. Thus she was frequently used to transport members of the Royal Family to and from the Isle of Wight. In this service she replaced *Osborne* (1st), referred to below. She was sometimes used by the then Prince of Wales (later King Edward VII) and Princess (Queen) Alexandra on cruises to the Baltic and Mediterranean. She was scrapped in 1908 after the turbine powered *Alexandra* was built.

Another *Osborne* preceded this one. Built as and christened *Victoria and Albert* (1st) her name was changed to *Osborne* (1st) in 1855 when the *Victoria and Albert* (2nd) was built. She was designed by Symonds and built at Pembroke Dockyard in 1845. She was 225′ LOA, with a gross tonnage of 1034. She was a paddle wheeler, with a speed of 11 knots. She was scrapped in 1868.

34

OSBORNE (2nd) ~ 1870

DEISGNER: *E. J. Reed*

BUILT: *1870*   BY *Pembroke Dockyard*

MATERIAL: RIG: *Paddle Schooner*

OWNERS
British Navy as Royal Yacht

LOA	LWL	BEAM	DRAFT in feet
284	*250*	*36.2*	*15.1*

GROSS TON	NET TON	TYM	DISP
1850		*1490*	*1850*

POWER: BOILER   ENGINE
   Scotch   *Paddle*

BHP (TOTAL)   SPEED (KNOTS)
   3360 IHP   *15.0*

SUNBEAM ~ 1874

DESIGNER: *St. Clair Byrne*
BUILT: *1874* By *Bowlder & Chaffers, Seacombe*
MATERIAL: *Composite—*   RIG: *3 Masted Topsail*
         Iron Frames   *Schooner*

LOA	LWL	BEAM	DRAFT in feet
170	154.7	27.6	13.5

GROSS TON	NET TON	TYM	DISP
334	227	532	

POWER: BOILER   ENGINE
      1 Scotch   *1 Comp. 24 × 42/21*

BHP (TOTAL)   SPEED (KNOTS)
   350 IHP   *10.3*

OWNERS:
Thomas Brassey (Earl Brassey) 1874–1916, 1919
Royal Indian Marine 1916–1919
Devitt & Moore 1920–1922
Walter Runciman (later Lord Runciman) 1922–1929)

36

Sunbeam was probably the best known steam yacht in the history of English yachting. She lived to a ripe age of 55 years. Her extensive cruising was engagingly described by Mrs. (later Lady) Brassey in several books, which could be found all over the world. Her owner, who acted as her master for nearly 45 years and who was active in promoting a strong Naval Reserve, was a prominent man. All this, along with her seaworthy appearing qualities, gave to *Sunbeam* a fame, a love, unsurpassed by any other yacht.

Thomas Brassey was the son of Thomas Brassey, the greatest railway contractor of his era. He cruised on several sail and steam yachts and made one transatlantic trip before he built *Sunbeam* in 1874. He cruised in her, until 1916 when she became a hospital ship, for over 500,000 miles. His cruises included not only the celebrated round-the-world voyage of 1876–1877, but also three to the United States and the West Indies, including the Kaiser's Cup race of 1905, two to Canada, three to India, and two to Australia. There were of course many shorter cruises to the Mediterranean, Ireland, Scotland, Norway, etc.

Thomas Brassey eventually became Earl Brassey, so he will be referred to hereafter as Lord Brassey. Though he had a sailing master, he was his own captain and navigator, in an era when few owners had anything to do with the management of their yachts. It was the great age of professional yacht captains and crews. *Sunbeam*, of course, had a complete professional crew that, at the start of her round-the-world voyage, totalled 32, comprising sailing master, boatswain, carpenter, and fourteen hands, four in the engine room and eleven among stewards, cooks, kitchen help, maids and nanny.

A brief resumé of her round-the-world voyage may be of interest as it was one of the first by a yacht and certainly the first of an entire family including small children. They started on July 1, 1876, after *Sunbeam* had had shakedown trips. Aboard were Mr. and Mrs. Brassey, a grown-up son, Allnutt, and three young daughters; also a doctor, an artist, and for the first part of the voyage, the celebrated Captain Lecky, author of "Wrinkles of Practical Navigation." They had a pleasant trip to Rio (interrupted by sighting and boarding a derelict loaded with wine), and visits to Madeira, the Canaries, and the Cape Verde islands. Mrs. Brassey's book is full of fascinating descriptions of people, places, and towns, all from the fresh view of a most observant yet unseasoned traveler. She describes homes, conveyances, etc., of over 100 years ago. It is delightful to read her comments on places that one knows so many years later. It is hard for us to realize that in that day, classified advertisements in the Rio de Janeiro newspapers offered, in Portuguese and English, slaves for sale with descriptions of their attractions and abilities similar to those in adjoining ads offering Singer sewing machines or pianos or harness.

Among the railways built by Thomas Brassey's father, there were many in South America built at the contractor's expense but including extensive land and property rights. Several of these were in Brazil, Argentina, and Chile. The Brasseys visited many of these properties inherited from his father. For those who know Buenos Aires now, even in *Sunbeam*'s time she had to anchor several miles offshore while passengers as well as cargo from freighters had to be taken to the shallow shore, where another transshipment was made into huge high-wheeled bullock carts to go ashore. Brassey's railway system in Argentina was so extensive that it has hardly been improved upon nearly a century later. Its excellence has actually hindered the development of roads in the interior.

From Buenos Aires, *Sunbeam* headed for the Pacific by the Straits of Magellan. En route, they encountered the bark *Monkshaven* with her cargo of smelting coal afire. Soon after her crew were rescued, she burst into flames and sank. In the straits, *Sunbeam* encountered Fuegian Indians. At that time they were of a low order of intelligence. Even in the desolate, rainy, foggy, terrible windy, raw climate, the Indians had not learned the art of making clothes or houses, but existed naked protected by a guanaco (llama family) skin wrapped around them or propped up as a lean-to against the raw prevailing winds.

Sunbeam then visited Valparaiso, Chile, before crossing the Pacific to the Taumatomos and Tahiti. Mrs. Brassey's descriptions of Tahiti show that it hardly changed until the arrival of the airplane in post-World War II days. *Sunbeam* even had the crew trouble that has plagued yachts to this day. Hilo, Honolulu, and Yokohama followed. Tokyo, now the largest city in the world and one of the most modern, was, in 1877, a purely Japanese city, with not one foreigner (except for the ministries that were inside the walled citadel). There was not one hotel in Tokyo, a far cry from the present. *Sunbeam* carried the Brasseys through the Inland Sea in midwinter and continued southward to Hong Kong, Canton, Macao, Singapore, Penang, Ceylon, Aden, Suez, Malta, and Lisbon to their home of Hastings, England, where they arrived on May 27, 1877.

That voyage covered 425 days of which 112 were spent in port. Of the total of 35,375 miles, 14,979 were under steam and 20,396 under sail. Her best day's run under sail was 299 miles and under steam 230 miles. The highest speed of 15 knots was reached in a squall in the North Pacific.

Most of the crew came from Essex, England. A majority were related in one way or another to the sail-

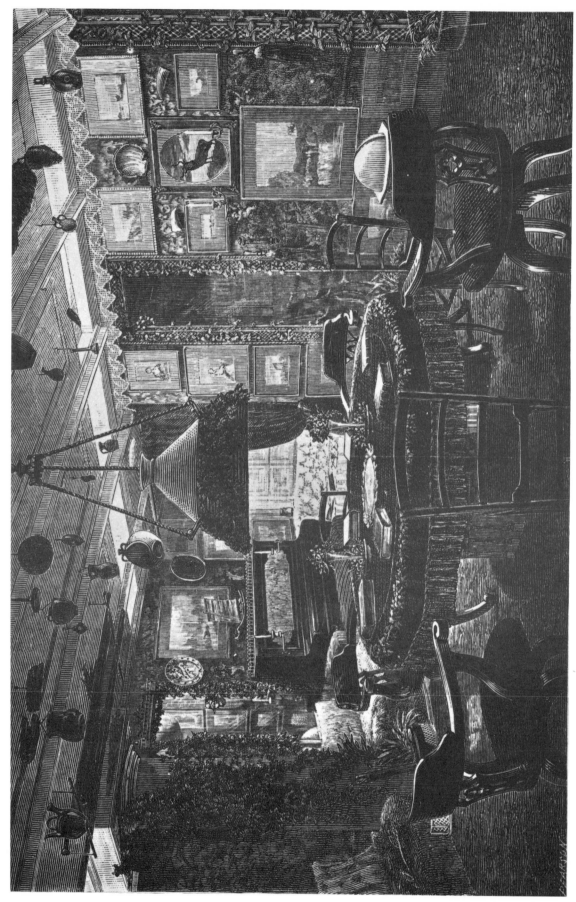

SUNBEAM DINING SALOON

38

ing master Powell, and all belonged to families that had been coastal fishermen for generations. Thus the voyage was, to a considerable extent, a family affair.

Sunbeam's voyages to North America were anti-climactic except for her entry in the Kaiser's Cup transatlantic race of 1905. Because of her fame and the charm of her owner/captain, she was a favorite (not to win) of the race, won, of course, by the great schooner *Atlantic* in the record time of 12 days, 4.1 hours. *Sunbeam*, the square-rigged ship *Valhalla*, and the bark *Apache* did not fare so well under the existing conditions. Of her two voyages to Australia, one was via Suez and the other via the Cape of Good Hope. While on a cruise around Australia in 1887, Lady Brassey died aboard *Sunbeam*. In 1895 Lord Brassey became Governor of Victoria (Australia) and so went out on *Sunbeam's* second voyage to Australia. Her voyages to Canada (1910) and India (1913–1914) were her last under Lord Brassey until he delivered her to India in 1916 to become a hospital ship.

After World War I she was bought by Lord Runciman, ship owner, who cruised in her until she had to be scrapped in 1929 after 55 years of cruising.

In her book "Sunshine and Storm in the Far East," Mrs. Brassey says that in 1878 *Sunbeam's* mate and chief engineer were paid £3–4 per week and found. Steward and cook received about £1/10 to 2/0, also found, while carpenter and quartermasters got 28/0, and seamen around 26/0 per week out of which they fed themselves! That year *Sunbeam* had two mates (Brassey was his own master), storekeeper, carpenter, quartermaster, five coxswains, one lamptrimmer, six seamen, with two engineers, four stewards, three cooks, one boy, and three stewardess/nurses.

Interestingly Lord Brassey's brother owned the three-masted topsail schooner *Czarina* (564 TYM) which was rather similiar in appearance to *Sunbeam. Czarina*, built in 1875, became a commercial vessel in World War I and was torpedoed and sunk in the Bay of Biscay.

CORSAIR (1st) ~ 1880

Other Names
KANAPHA

DESIGNER: *Wm. Cramp & Sons*
BUILT: *1880* BY *Wm. Cramp & Sons*
MATERIAL: *Iron*   RIG: *Screw Schooner*

LOA	LWL	BEAM	DRAFT in feet
189	165	23.7	10.5

GROSS TON	NET TON	TYM	DISP
247	124	486	

POWER: BOILER   ENGINE
         2 Scotch   *1 Comp.24 × 44/24*

BHP (TOTAL)   SPEED (KNOTS)
                          14.0

OWNERS:
C. J. Osborn 1880–1882
J. Pierpont Morgan 1882–1890
Rev. W. V. Moore 1890–1898 (Kanapha)

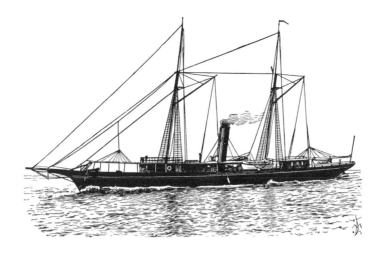

Corsair and her sister yacht *Stranger* were among the first large steam yachts built in the United States. There may be some confusion between the two yachts as their owners' names were so similar, Osborn and Osgood. *Stranger* eventually went into the US Navy.

J. Pierpont Morgan, having chartered a yacht, bought *Corsair*. He used her mainly to commute between his home up the Hudson River and New York City. He enjoyed the peace and comfort of this form of transportation so much that a few years later he had a larger yacht, also named *Corsair*, built to his own needs. Thus the first *Corsair* was notable primarily as Mr. Morgan's introduction to yachting.

This *Corsair*, later called *Kanapha*, was chartered by the press to carry dispatches from the war zone in Cuba to Key West for transmittal by wire to the newspapers. She was lost in this service off Cape Maysi, at the eastern end of Cuba, in 1898.

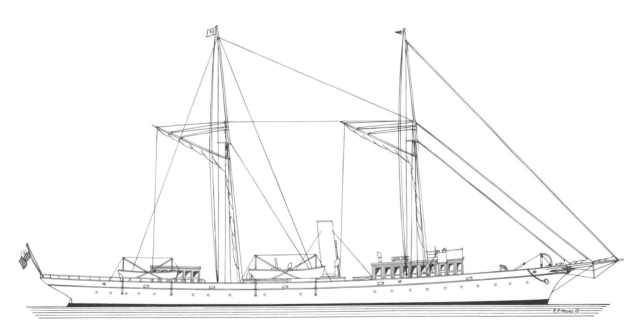

41

Livadia was one of the most unusual yachts ever built, and it is a pity her active service was so brief. Vice-Admiral Popoff of the Russian Navy had designed and built several circular ironclad batteries to achieve a shallow-draft, steady platform for large cannon. They were fairly successful, so a floating home was built for Czar Alexander II. It was hoped that her steadiness would cause a revolution in passenger ship design.

In profile she had a pleasant yacht-like appearance, but head on one could see her very wide superstructure mounted on a hull far wider amidships. She resembled some later warships with exaggerated anti-torpedo blisters or bulges. She was triple screw with three funnels abreast. A separate walkway around the hull, mounted above the bulges on columns, gave access to the boats, line handling parties, etc. Popoff's principle was to provide a steady platform while the rounded edges of the bulges would permit waves to run off harmlessly. On her voyage to the Black Sea, she met a gale in the Bay of Biscay. She was rock steady as far as rolling or pitching was concerned, but her area of flat bottom pounded in a terrifying manner, so hard that she stove in some of her well-compartmented double bottom, and had to go into El Ferrol, Spain. As there was no drydock in the world that could handle a vessel of over 150′ beam in those days, Fairfield, her builder, had to construct a cofferdam around her. She eventually reached the Black Sea. Shortly afterward, the Czar was assassinated. A new Royal Yacht was built and *Livadia* was laid up. She remained through wars and revolutions in Sevastopol until she was finally broken up as recently as 1926.

Apart from her unique design, her interior was said to be most luxurious, and roomy due to her great beam. The Imperial quarters had 12′ head room. Corridors in the Imperial quarters were floored in marble, while the grand salon had a fountain surrounded by a flower bed.

LIVADIA ~ 1880

DESIGNER: *Vice-Adm. Popoff*
BUILT: *1880* BY *Fairfield SB Eng. Co.*
MATERIAL: *Steel*   RIG:

LOA	LWL	BEAM	DRAFT in feet
260		*153*	*16.5*

GROSS TON	NET TON	TYM	DISP
11600			*4000*

POWER: BOILER   ENGINE
        3 Scotch   *3 Comp. 60 × 78 × 78/39*
BHP (TOTAL)   SPEED (KNOTS)
   7000   *16½*

OWNERS:
*Russian Government as Imperial Yacht for Czar
   Alexander—later laid up*

43

NAMOUNA ~ 1882

Other Names
GENERAL PINZON

DESIGNER: *St. Clair Byrne*
BUILT: *1882* By *Ward Stanton & Co., Newburgh*
MATERIAL: *Iron*   RIG: *Screw Schooner*

LOA	LWL	BEAM	DRAFT in feet
247	217	26.4	14.4

GROSS TON	NET TON	TYM	DISP
616	308	740	

POWER: BOILER   ENGINE
    1 Scotch   *1 Comp. 22 × 42/28*
        changed to TE 21 × 34 × 55/30 in 1893

OWNERS:
James Gordon Bennett 1882–1900
Columbian Navy 1901–

44

James Gordon Bennett was one of the few yachtsmen of his era who enjoyed and participated in ocean sailing and racing. Son of the owner of the New York Herald, he became a member of the New York Yacht Club. His father gave him a sloop and arranged for the great "Bully" Samuels, former master of the clipper packet *Dreadnaught*, to teach him sailing. Bennett had a schooner, *Henrietta*, built in 1861. Together Bennett and *Henrietta* served in the Navy during the Civil War. In 1866 a wager among three schooner owners resulted in the first transatlantic race, run in December. The other owners were content to stay in the warmth of their clubs, but Bennett and the redoubtable Samuels raced *Henrietta* across to win in the respectable time of 13 days, 22 hours to the Needles, or an average of 9.2 knots. Naturally the race and the winner were duly covered by the New York Herald.

Later Bennett built *Dauntless*, another well-known schooner. He raced her across the Atlantic against *Cambria*, which was headed for a challenge for the America's Cup, but lost by 1 hour, 17 minutes. After an interval, succumbing to the pleasures of steam power because few guests enjoyed his hard-driving sailing, he built the luxurious *Namouna*. She was referred to, undoubtedly in the Herald, as the "first floating palace." Bennett, now owner of the remarkably successful Herald, spent a good deal of the time aboard *Namouna* in New York or in France, where he lived more and more of the time. He would travel back and forth on *Namouna*. He was the despair of members of the Herald, who might be interviewed for an hour, or might be taken without warning on a voyage to Europe or elsewhere.

Namouna served Bennett well for 18 years until he built the far larger and even more luxurious yacht *Lysistrata*. *Namouna* ended her life in the Columbian Navy.

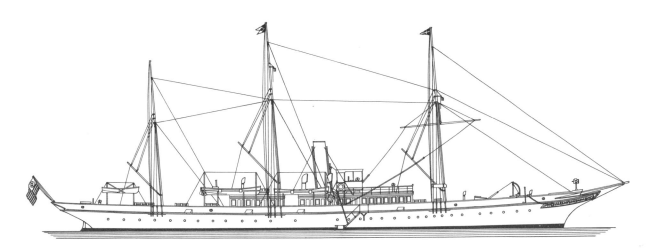

ATALANTA ~ 1883

Other Names
RESTAURADOR
GENERAL SALOM

DESIGNER: *Wm. Cramp & Sons*
BUILT: *1883*   BY *Wm. Cramp & Sons*
MATERIAL: *Iron*   RIG: *Screw Schooner*

LOA	LWL	BEAM	DRAFT in feet
°250.3	233.3	26.4	13.0

GROSS TON	NET TON	TYM	DISP
568	284		750

POWER: BOILER   ENGINE
        2 Scotch   *1 Comp 30 × 60/30*

BHP (TOTAL)	SPEED (KNOTS)
1750	17

OWNERS:
Jay Gould, George Gould 1883–1902
*Venezuelan Navy 1902–1950 (Restaurador, General
   Salom)*

°Lengthened 15' early in life. Length shown is final one.

Atalanta was a fast yacht for her time, but her coal capacity was limited and on transatlantic trips she had to go via the Azores for coaling. The Goulds made several trips to England in her, and the photo shown appears to have been taken up the Medina River in Cowes. Her owner challenged several other yachts to races without results until he raced the Herreshoff-built *Vamoose* off New York and, as expected, was soundly beaten. After all, Hearst's *Vamoose* was a high-speed commuter. It is too bad that he didn't try to race the more comparable *Kanahwa*.

She was sold to the Venezuelan Navy in 1902. She was rebuilt in 1938 and was finally dropped from Jane's in 1950 after 67 years of service.

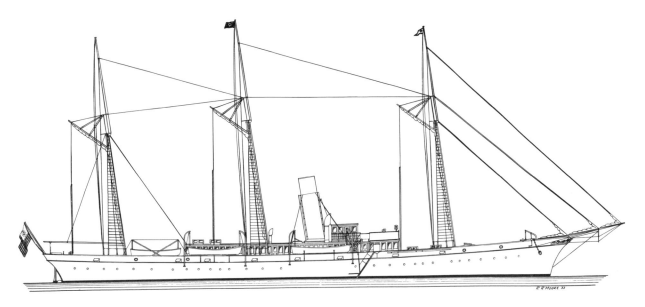

ELECTRA ~ 1884

DESIGNER: *Gustav Hillman*
BUILT: *1884*   By: *Harlan & Hollingsworth*
MATERIAL *Iron*   RIG: *Screw Schooner*

LOA	LWL	BEAM	DRAFT in feet
173	*161.4*	*23.0*	*10.0*

GROSS TON	NET TON	TYM	DISP
316	*215*	*422*	

POWER: BOILER   ENGINE
        2 Water-tube   *1 Comp. 26 × 46/26*
                              1 TE 19 × 28 × 42/24 in 1897

BHP: (TOTAL)   SPEED (KNOTS)

OWNERS:
Elbridge T. Gerry 1884–1912

48

Electra was one of several yachts built in the US by Harlan & Hollingsworth of Wilmington, Delaware. She was one of the first, if not the first, fitted with electric lighting. This comprised 58 16-candlepower lights plus a 100-candlepower searchlight, all installed by Edison. Her greatest call to fame was her ice-making plant, the first on a yacht. It made all of 56 pounds of ice per day, hardly enough to cool the champagne. Regardless of that, *Electra* served the Gerry family well for nearly 30 years before she was broken up in 1912, under one ownership throughout her life.

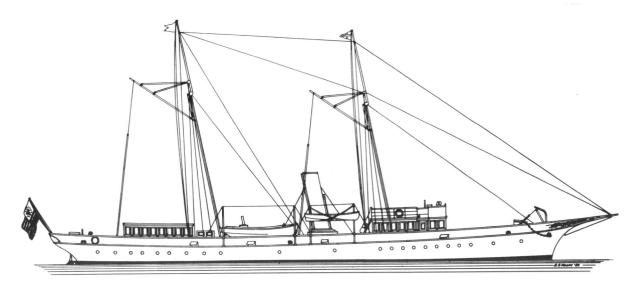

NOURMAHAL ~ 1884

DESIGNER: *Gustav Hillman*
BUILT: *1884* By: *Harlan & Hollingsworth*
MATERIAL: *Steel*   RIG: *Screw Bark*

LOA	LWL	BEAM	DRAFT in feet
250	221	30	14.3

GROSS TON	NET TON	TYM	DISP
750	373	939	

POWER: BOILER   ENGINE
     4 Scotch   *1 Comp. 34 × 60/36*
BHP (TOTAL)   SPEED (KNOTS)

OWNERS: *William Astor, J. J. Astor 1884–1909*
Pierre Demers 1910–1913
Brazilianische Bank fur Deutschland (no longer a yacht)

Nourmahal was another of the Hillman/H&H yachts and one of the first yachts owned by members of the Astor family, who in succeeding years became great yacht owners. Lloyd's notes that her rig was changed from a bark to a schooner in 1902. She was sold to German interests early in World War I.

Nourmahal had successors. One, designed by Gardner & Cox in 1901, was evidently never built. She would have been a spar-decked yacht, 280 × 227 × 32 × 13. Another was designed by Cox & Stevens and built by Robert Jacob in 1920. She was a diesel yacht 160′ LOA and 418 TYM. She later became "*Alder*." During World War II she entered the Canadian Navy, became HMCS *Otter*, and was lost in 1941. The other *Nourmahal* and by far the best known was designed by Theodore Ferris and built by Krupp in 1928. She was diesel-powered, 264′ LOA, and 2036 TYM. During World War II she went into the US Navy and Coast Guard. She was broken up in August, 1965.

ALVA ~ 1885

DESIGNER: *St. Clair Byrne*
BUILT: *1885* By: *Harlan & Hollingsworth*
MATERIAL: *Steel*   RIG: *3 Masted Topsail*
                          Schooner

OWNERS:
W. K. Vanderbilt 1885–1892

LOA	LWL	BEAM	DRAFT in feet
285	*252*	*32*	*16.8*

GROSS TON	NET TON	TYM	DISP
1151	*601*	*1238*	*1300*

POWER: BOILER   ENGINE
     2 Scotch   *1 Comp. 32 × 45 × 45/42*

BHP (TOTAL)   SPEED (KNOTS)
                      14

Alva was one of the first large steel seagoing yachts built in the United States, though her designer, St. Clair Byrne, was one of the more experienced British designers. Her owner, very proud of her, claimed that the only foreign material used in her construction was the Russian hemp in her rigging and lines.

Her cost, even in those days, was reported to be about $500,000, more costly than if she had been built in Great Britain. Her upkeep, including wages for her crew of 53, came to $5,000 per month in 1886.

Unfortunately she was sunk in a collision off Martha's Vineyard in 1892. Even though she sank in shallow water she was not repaired.

Another *Alva*, a diesel yacht, 264' LOA and 2305 TYM, designed by Cox & Stevens, was built by Krupp in 1931. As the USS *Plymouth*, she was torpedoed off the North Carolina coast in 1942.

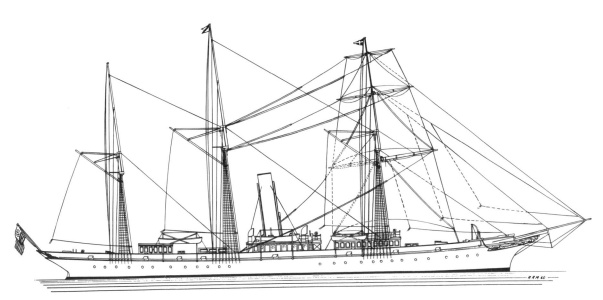

STILETTO ~ 1883

Other Names:
TORPEDO BOAT No. 2 (USS

DESIGNER: *N. G. Herreshoff*
BUILT: *1885* By *Herreshoff Mfg. Co.*
MATERIAL: *Wood*   RIG: *Screw Schooner*

LOA	LWL	BEAM	DRAFT in feet
94	*90*	*11.2*	*4.6*

GROSS TON	NET TON	TYM	DISP
46	*24*		

POWER: BOILER   ENGINE
         1 Water-tube   *1 Comp 12 × 21/12*

BHP (TOTAL)	SPEED (KNOTS)
450 IHP	*23*

OWNERS:
Herreshoff Mfg. Co. 1885–1887
US Navy 1887–1911

54

Stiletto was built by the Herreshoffs to show their design of a really high speed steam craft, and particularly their boiler and engine design. She was probably the first high-speed craft in the United States. Her Herreshoff boiler, a water-tube model, was somewhat between a normal coil boiler and the three-drum type that later became almost standard for high-speed vessels. Her speed was phenomenal for that era. She made one 8 hour test run at 26½ miles per hour (23 knots). Her fame rested more on a run with the Hudson River Liner *Mary Powell*, known as the fastest steamer in the United States. On June 10, 1885, *Stiletto*, handled by N. G. Herreshoff, met the *Mary Powell*. She ran alongside for a few miles, then speeded up to ahead of the *Mary Powell*. From that position she crossed her bow, slowed to let *Mary Powell* pass, then opened up, overhauling, passing, and going ahead again. It was a convincing demonstration and one that won a great deal of fame for Herreshoff. Because, or as a result, of her

fame, *Stiletto* was sold to the US Navy in 1887 to be a torpedo boat. She remained in naval service until 1911.

The first torpedo boat in the US Navy was *Lightning*, also built by Herreshoff, 1875. *Lightning* was 58' long with a speed of 22 knots. She carried a "spar" torpedo or torpedoes mounted on a spar projecting ahead of the boat, and attacked by ramming the sparred torpedo into an enemy vessel. After the *Lightning*, Herreshoff built several more small torpedo boats: USS *Cushing* (140' LOA), USS *Du Pont* (176' LOA) and her sister USS *Porter*, USS *Morris* (140' LOA), and the sisters USS *Gwin* (100' LOA) and USS *Talbot*. Growing interference in the design and construction of these excellent craft by Navy inspectors induced the independent Herreshoff brothers to withdraw from further interest in designs for the Navy. Unfortunately both the Herreshoffs and the Navy lost by such intransigency on both sides.

NOW THEN ~ 1887

DESIGNER: *N. G. Herreshoff*
BUILT: *1887* By *Herreshoff Mfg. Co.*
MATERIAL: *Wood*   RIG: *Screw Schooner*
LOA   LWL   BEAM   DRAFT in feet
 92   80
GROSS TON   NET TON   TYM   DISP

POWER: BOILER   ENGINE
     1 Water-tube   *1 TE*
BHP (TOTAL)   SPEED (KNOTS)
                   21

OWNERS:
Norman Munro 1887–1888

Now Then, built for Norman Munro, a New York publisher, was the forerunner of fast commuting craft. She retained characteristics in appearance that made her very old-fashioned looking for an up-to-date yacht, clipper bow, two masts, and worst of all, an exaggerated "beavertail" stern. This stern gave the then believed appearance of speed, but was an abomination when backing as it scooped up water onto the deck aft. But she was fast. On her initial delivery trip she went from Newport, Rhode Island to New York (170 statute miles) in 7 hours, 40 minutes, or at a speed of over 24 statute miles per hour.

BALLYMENA ~ 1888

Other Names
BELLEMERE

DESIGNER: *N. G. Herreshoff*
BUILT: *1888* BY *Herreshoff Mfg. Co.*
MATERIAL: *Steel*   RIG: *Screw Schooner*

LOA	LWL	BEAM	DRAFT in feet
148	*133*	*17.7*	*8.0*

GROSS TON	NET TON	TYM	DISP
146	*73*	*197*	

POWER: BOILER   ENGINE
      1 Water-tube   *1 QE 11¼ × 16 × 22½ ×*
                       22½ × 22½ × /15

BHP (TOTAL)   SPEED (KNOTS)
   875

OWNERS:
Alexander Brown 1888–1894 (est.)
J. Nicholas Brown 1894–1900
S. T. Shaw 1901–1906 (Bellemere)
Roy Rainey 1907–1908
Mrs. H. N. Slater 1909–1913
C. R. Nedlinger 1914
Commercial interests 1915

I believe that *Ballymena* was the first steel yacht built by Herreshoff. She was powered with one of the five well-known five-cylinder quadruple expansion engines built by Herreshoff. Like most Herreshoff craft she lasted for many years.

She went into commercial service under the Honduras flag in 1915.

59

LADY TORFRIDA ~ 1888

Other Names
VALFREYIA
STAR OF INDIA

DESIGNER: *Fairfield SB & Eng. Co.*
BUILT: *1888* BY *Fairfield SB & Eng. Co.*
MATERIAL: *Steel* RIG: *Screw Schooner*

LOA	LWL	BEAM	DRAFT in feet
234	208.7	27.0	15.0

GROSS TON	NET TON	TYM	DISP
545	304	735	

POWER: BOILER ENGINE
  1 Scotch, Oil in 1932 *1 TE 14¼ × 14¼ ×*
   30½ × 38 × 38/30

BHP (TOTAL) SPEED (KNOTS)
  1400 IHP

OWNERS:
Sir William Pearce 1888–1890
Bayard Brown 1890–1927 (Valfreyia)
Maharajah of Nawanagar 1928–1929 (Star of India)
Maharajah of Patiala 1929–1930
Sir George Hutchinson 1931
Sir Wyndham Portal (Later Lord Portal) 1932–1939
British Navy World War II

This yacht was rather well known, first as one of the confusing family of *Lady Torfridas* referred to below; secondly because of her static life for so many years when owned by Mr. Brown as referred to in the text; and thirdly for her rejuvenation under Indian ownership. In World War II she served in the British Navy as an accommodation ship, but as stated in the text she missed service in World War I because her maintenance had been so poor that the Admiralty, desperate for vessels, had to refuse her at that time. She was not listed in Lloyd's after 1947.

There has always been some confusion as there were two other *Lady Torfridas*, both also built by Fairfield for their Director, Sir William Pearce. The first was 623 TYM and built in 1883. She was later called *Tamara*. The second was the present subject. The third was 543 TYM and was built in 1890. She remained *Lady Torfrida*.

This photograph, taken when she was *Star of India*, shows her modernized, evidently after her years of neglect as *Valfreyia*.

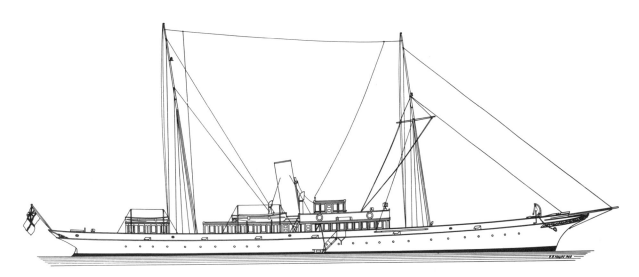

SAY WHEN ~ 1888

DESIGNER: *N. G. Herreshoff*
BUILT: *1888* BY *Herreshoff Mfg. Co.*
MATERIAL: *Composite* RIG: *Screw Schooner*

LOA	LWL	BEAM	DRAFT in feet
138	115	14.0	4.5

GROSS TON	NET TON	TYM	DISP
87	44		

POWER: BOILER   ENGINE
  1 Water-tube 1 QE $11\frac{1}{4} \times 16 \times 22\frac{1}{2} \times$
              $22\frac{1}{2} \times 22\frac{1}{2}/15$

BHP (TOTAL)	SPEED (KNOTS)
875	21

OWNERS:
Norman Munro 1888
J. T. Blandford 1889–1891
W. J. White 1891–1908
F. K. Burnham 1909–1914

Say When followed the smaller *Now Then*, both built by Herreshoff for Norman Munro, a publisher. *Now Then's* forward-sloping stern was unsatisfactory as it scooped water onto the deck when reversing, so *Say When* had a normal counter stern. She was powered with one of the well-known Herreshoff five-cylinder, quadruple expansion engines.

She was not listed in Lloyd's after 1914.

SEMIRAMIS ~ 1889

Other Names
MARGARITA
NARADA

DESIGNER: *A. H. Brown*
BUILT: *1889* BY *Ramage & Ferguson*
MATERIAL: *Steel*   RIG: *Screw Brigantine*

LOA	LWL	BEAM	DRAFT in feet
225	194	27.2	13.0

GROSS TON	NET TON	TYM	DISP
491	272	703	

POWER: BOILER   ENGINE
    1 Scotch   *1 TE 18 × 29 × 47/33*

BHP (TOTAL)	SPEED (KNOTS)
635 IHP	14

OWNERS:
John Lysaght 1889–1893
Mme. Lebaudy 1893–1894
A. J. Drexel 1894–1899 (Margarita)
Henry Walters 1899–1933 (Narada)
US Navy World War I
Commercial interests 1933–

This is one of those yachts with two changes of name, both alike, that bedevil historians. She was one of the first designs of a former sailing ship master who turned to yacht design, and in his case was successful. He was widely known as "Skipper" Brown. She was a good, reliable, typical steam yacht of the period. She was eventually owned by Henry Walters of Baltimore. As "Narada" she became one of the best known yachts on the Atlantic. Her owner used her a great deal, and on her, made many trips to Europe, gathering art treasures that now form the basis of the Walters Art Gallery in Baltimore.

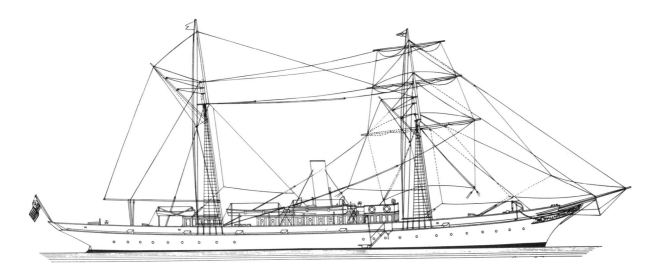

CORSAIR (2nd) ~ 1890

Other Names:
USS GLOUCESTER

DESIGNER: *J. Beavor–Webb*
BUILT: *1890*   By: *Neafie & Levy*
MATERIAL: *Steel*   RIG : *Screw Schooner*

LOA	LWL	BEAM	DRAFT in feet
241.5	204	27.0	13.0

GROSS TON	NET TON	TYM	DISP
560	280		

POWER: BOILER   ENGINE
         2 Scotch   *1 TE 21 × 33 × 54/30*

BHP (TOTAL)	SPEED (KNOTS)
2000	17

OWNERS:
J. Pierpont Morgan 1890–1898
US Navy 1898–1919 (USS Gloucester)

Except for *Corsair* (1st) all three others have become among the most famous yachts in United States history, and all three were involved in naval service. This yacht, the second *Corsair* (they were all *Corsair*, not *Corsair* II, III, IV), achieved the most publicized war career of the three.

Corsair (2nd) was built for J. Pierpont Morgan, after he had had eight years of experience with her predecessor. She was considerably larger to provide her owner with the princely comfort he desired. He used her a great deal, almost as another of his homes: 219 Madison Ave., New York, Princes Gate, London, or Dover House in the English countryside. He was elected Commodore of the New York Yacht Club in 1897. *Corsair* served as a notable flagship. He took a very active interest in the club, donated prizes, led the annual cruises in *Corsair*. Except for her lack of maneuverability due to her single screw, she fulfilled his wishes.

In April, 1898, he sold her to the US Navy for $225,000. The Navy converted her to a dispatch vessel and patrol gunboat, named her USS *Gloucester*, and put Lt. Comdr. Richard Wainwright, late of the USS *Maine*, in command. When Admiral Cervera's Spanish fleet was found in the protected harbor of Santiago de Cuba, USS *Gloucester* joined the blockading fleet. She moved in the sortie of the four cruis-

ers and two destroyers and attacked the second destroyer, *Pluton*, vastly superior a war vessel, driving her ashore to be abandoned. After the other Spanish ships had been driven ashore and afire, the *Gloucester* moved in to rescue many of their crews including Admiral Cervera himself.

Later on, USS *Gloucester*, alone, entered the defended harbor of Guanica, Puerto Rico. With her puny 3- and 6-pound cannon she silenced the batteries while her landing party was put ashore and captured the town, holding it until the United States land force could occupy it. At the end of the conflict USS *Gloucester* returned to the United States and made a triumphant visit to Gloucester, Massachusetts.

In the meantime, Mr. Morgan had built the third *Corsair*. The *Gloucester* spent many more years in the US Navy. In 1909 she was lent to the New York Naval Militia as a training vessel. During World War I she reverted to the Navy and operated near New York. She was sold out of the Navy in 1919, and in commercial service, she was wrecked in a hurricane at Pensacola, Florida.

Her first commanding officer went on to become a distinguished admiral, and in all naval histories covering the Spanish-American War, the USS *Gloucester* is recalled with the greatest honor and respect.

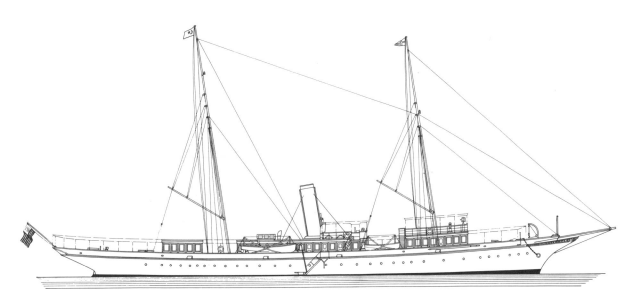

VAMOOSE ~ 1890

DESIGNER: *N. G. Herreshoff*
BUILT: *1890* BY: *Herreshoff Mfg. Co.*
MATERIAL: *Composite*   RIG: *Screw Steamer*

LOA	LWL	BEAM	DRAFT in feet
112.5	109.4	12.4	7.0

GROSS TON	NET TON	TYM	DISP
63	32		

POWER: BOILER   ENGINE
     1Water-tube $1\ QE11\tfrac{1}{4} \times 16 \times 22\tfrac{1}{2} \times$
                         $22\tfrac{1}{2} \times 22\tfrac{1}{2}/15$
          Gas engine installed in 1910

BHP (TOTAL)	SPEED (KNOTS)
875	23

OWNERS:
W. R. Hearst 1890–1893
Norman Munro 1894
F. T. Morrill 1894–1901
Howard Gould 1902
Walter Lewisohn 1903–1910
J. D. Maxwell 1910–1917
J. A. Pugh 1918–1921

Vamoose, like *Say When* and *Ballymena*, was one of the early Herreshoff express cruisers. Smaller than the other two, yet powered, as they were, with one of the five cylinder quadruple expansion engines (the other two were in the torpedo boat USS *Cushing*), she was a bit faster than the other yachts. Like other express cruisers she was used mainly for commuting and other services in Long Island Sound. She lasted over 30 years, a long life for a craft built as light as possible. She was not listed in Lloyd's after 1921.

WHITE HEATHER ~ 1890

Other Names:
APACHE

DESIGNER: *J. Reid & Co.*
BUILT: *1890* BY: *J. Reid & Co.*
MATERIAL: *Steel*   RIG: *Screw Bark*

LOA	LWL	BEAM	DRAFT in feet
198	168	28.2	13.0

GROSS TON	NET TON	TYM	DISP
443	240	635	

POWER: BOILER   ENGINE
    1 Scotch (Oil in 1914)   1 TE 13 × 21 × 34/27
BHP (TOTAL)   SPEED (KNOTS)

OWNERS:
R. Cecil Leigh 1890–1899
C. G. Millar 1900–1901
H. L. Drummond 1902–1903
Edmund Randolph 1904–1910 (Apache)
L. Legru 1910–1915 (not listed in Lloyd's, believed in French Navy in World War I)
Commercial interests 1919–

Though she was built as and long known as *White Heather*, this yacht is probably better known as *Apache*. She was a handsome and seaworthy vessel. She was one of the contestants in the Kaiser's Cup race in 1905. With her bark rig she needed strong winds. These she certainly did not get even though she took a northerly route. After many days of light winds she got her wind in gale force, but from ahead, which her square rig could not use. On top of these troubles she, on her northerly course, was not sighted for many days, resulting in rumors that she had been lost. She finished last, nearly four days after the next-to-last yacht.

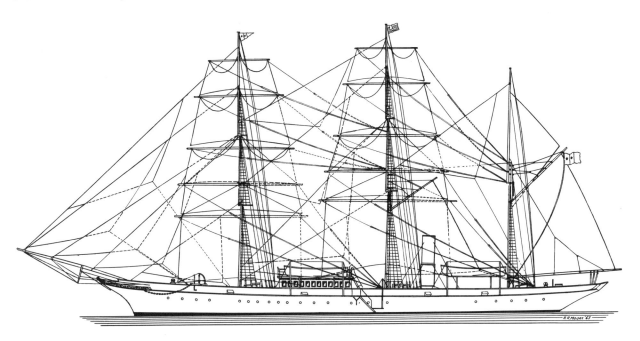

MAY ~ 1891

DESIGNER: *G. L. Watson*

BUILT: *1891* BY: *Ailsa SB & Eng. Co.*

MATERIAL: *Steel* RIG: *Screw Schooner*

LOA	LWL	BEAM	DRAFT in feet
240.0	203.8	27.8	14.4

GROSS TON	NET TON	TYM	DISP
653	369	766	

POWER: BROILER ENGINE
 1 Scotch *1 TE 19 × 31 × 51/33*

BHP (TOTAL) SPEED (KNOTS)

OWNERS:
Ninan B. Stewart 1891–1893
E. D. Morgan 1894–1896
Mrs. S. Drexel Fell 1897
A. van Rensselar 1898–1910
Walter F. Bliss 1911–1915
J. R. DeLamar 1916–1917
US Navy World War I

May was considered one of the best of Watson's designs and was often used as a standard of comparison for later craft of his design.

In 1916 her bowsprit and masts were replaced by a spike sprit and pole masts. The deck over her forward deckhouse was made continuous to the after end of her after deckhouse and was carried out to the sides of the vessel just aft of the bridge. The former bridge was replaced by a pilothouse and a flying bridge. Under Mr. Morgan she was flagship of the New York Yacht Club.

Unfortunately she was wrecked in the West Indies while in naval service in 1919.

73

CLERMONT ~ 1892

Other Names
CHARMARY

DESIGNER: *A. van Santvoord*
BUILT: *1892*   BY: *H. Lawrence, Greenpoint*
MATERIAL: *Wood*   RIG: *Paddle Schooner*

LOA	LWL	BEAM	DRAFT in feet
°175	165	43/25.5	5.6

GROSS TON	NET TON	TYM	DISP
299	203		

POWER: BOILER   ENGINE
      1 Scotch   *Paddle Beam 40/72*

BHP (TOTAL)   SPEED (KNOTS)
                    16

°*Lengthened 15' in 1897.*

OWNERS:
A. van Santvoord 1892–1903
Charles G. Gates 1904–1911
Commercial interests 1911–about 1921

Clermont was one of the few paddle yachts built after screw propellers came into service. She was designed by her owner, who was the principal owner and head of the Hudson River Day Line. This company operated excursion steamers for over 90 years. Among its fleet, nearly all paddle wheelers, was the *Mary Powell* (Queen of the Hudson River) which, though built in 1861, was the accepted standard for speed for generations. A fast yacht would always try to race the *Mary Powell*.

After several years as a yacht *Clermont* was converted into service as an excursion steamer on the Hudson River. She was dropped from Lloyd's as a yacht in 1912.

VALHALLA ~ 1892

DESIGNER: *W. C. Storey*
BUILT: *1892*   BY: *Ramage & Ferguson*
MATERIAL: *Steel*   RIG: *Aux. Screw 3 Masted Ship*

LOA	LWL	BEAM	DRAFT *in feet*
245	*208*	*37.3*	

GROSS TON	NET TON	TYM	DISP
1218	*806*	*1490*	

POWER: BOILER   ENGINE
        2 Scotch   *1 TE 18½ × 27¾ × 47/33*
BHP (TOTAL)   SPEED (KNOTS)

OWNERS:
Capt. J. F. Laycock 1892–1897
Comte Boni de Castellane 1898–1902
Earl of Crawford 1902–1908
Irving Cox 1909–1910
George Marvin 1911–1915
British Navy World War I
B. H. Clerc 1919
Commercial interests 1920–

I believe *Valhalla* and *American* were the only ship-rigged steam yachts, though there have been several others that were partially square-rigged, while *Seven Seas*, though ship-rigged, was diesel powered.

Valhalla is probably best known as a competitor in the Kaiser's Transatlantic Race in 1905. She, *Sunbeam*, and *Apache* were no match for the fast schooners in that race, but in spite of such a handicap *Valhalla* finished third after *Atlantic* and *Hamburg* in 14 days, 2 hours, and 53 minutes.

When owned by the Earl of Crawford, an enthusiastic scientist and ornithologist, she made several extended trips to catch rare birds. On one trip in particular, in 1905–1906, she went to the Indian Ocean and to Tristan da Cunha for birds. Her owner was also an astronomer of note and once voyaged to Mauritius to observe the transit of Venus.

During World War I she served as a floating workshop in the Royal Navy and for some time was stationed at Mudros Bay on the island of Limnos, the British base for the naval part of the Gallipoli campaign.

After the war she became a Spanish fruit carrier but foundered off Cape St. Vincent in 1922.

CLEOPATRA ~ 1893

Other Names:
SAPPHIRE
PENELOPE
USS YANKTON

DESIGNER: *G. L. Watson*
BUILT: *1893* BY: *Ramage & Ferguson*
MATERIAL: *Steel*   RIG: *Screw Schooner*

LOA	LWL	BEAM	DRAFT in feet
217	*185*	*27.5*	*13.8*

GROSS TON	NET TON	TYM	DISP
541	*272*	*675*	*975*

POWER: BOILER   ENGINE
      1 Scotch   *1 TE 18 × 29 × 47/33*

BHP (TOTAL)	SPEED (KNOTS)
750 IHP	*12½*

OWNERS:
John Lysaght 1893–1894
A. L. Barber 1895–1896 (Sapphire)
H. E. Converse 1897–1898 (Penelope)
US Navy 1898–1921 (USS Yankton)
Commercial interests 1921–1925

Cleopatra's initial cruise was to the Norwegian coast. After her owner died she was apparently chartered to the actress Sarah Bernhardt. It seems certain that she did not own *Cleopatra* as has been reported. A. L. Barber, of asphalt fame, bought her and sold her to Colonel Converse, who sold his yacht *Calypso* to Mr. Barber. At the time of the Spanish War she was sold to the US Navy and commissioned USS *Yankton*, as the name *Penelope* was not considered suitable for a naval vessel, though there have been several of that name in the Royal Navy. After serving in the war she became a survey vessel and then a tender to the At-

lantic Fleet. In World War I she served on east coast of the United States and in the Mediterranean. Returning to the United States, she was refitted for service in the Arctic, and was several months in the White Sea area before she returned home for decommissioning in 1921. From then on life was hard. She became a rumrunner and was hijacked. She later became a small passenger carrier-cum-freighter running between Boston and Canada's Maritime Provinces before running aground and wrecked in Boston harbor in January, 1925. She was finally broken up in 1930.

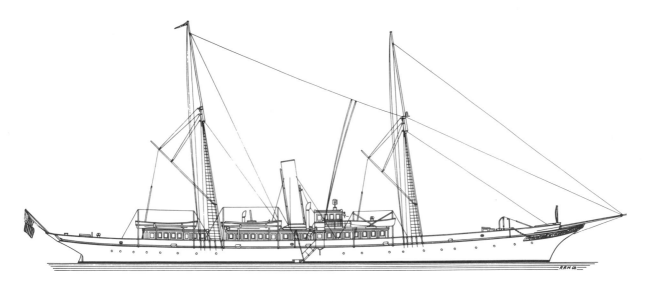

HOHENZOLLERN ~ 1893

DESIGNER: *German Admiralty*
BUILT: *1893* BY: *Vulcan-Stettin*
MATERIAL: *Steel*   RIG: *Twin Screw Schooner*

LOA	LWL	BEAM	DRAFT in feet
382.6	375	45.9	23.1

GROSS TON	NET TON	TYM	DISP
3756	2214	3773	

POWER: BOILER   ENGINE
   8 Scotch   *2 TE 36 × 58 × 93/37 each*
BHP (TOTAL)   SPEED (KNOTS)
 9000 IHP   *21.5*

OWNERS:
*German Admiralty for Imperial Royal Yacht but
 classed as dispatch ship*

When she was contemplated in the Naval Appropriation, the Socialists in the Reichstag would not approve funds for an Imperial Yacht, so the *Hohenzollern* was built as a dispatch boat, but taken over after completion and fitted out as the Imperial Yacht. She replaced an early paddle *Hohenzollern* built in 1875.

The Kaiser used her on many voyages to the Mediterranean and to the Baltic and Norwegian waters. He seldom missed the chance of being at Cowes for Cowes week, and of course was the center of attention at all Kiel weeks.

She made at least one trip to the United States, in 1902. She brought Prince Henry, the Kaiser's brother, for the launching and christening of the Kaiser's racing schooner *Meteor III*, designed by Cary Smith and built in the United States.

In 1913, a new and far larger Imperial Yacht was under construction (see *Ersatz Hohenzollern*) to replace her. World War I intervened, the new yacht was never completed, and with the abdication of the Kaiser there was no need for such a vessel. She was sold about 1920 and broken up in 1923.

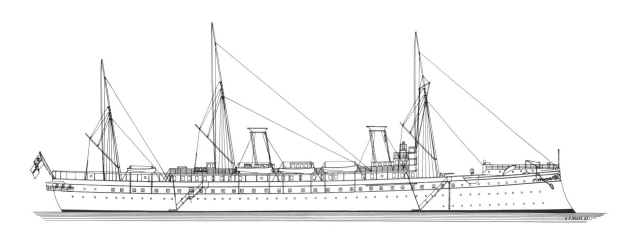

VALIANT ~ 1893

DESIGNER: *St. Clair Byrne*
BUILT: *1893* BY: *Laird, Birkenhead*
MATERIAL: *Steel*   RIG: *Twin Screw Brig*

LOA	LWL	BEAM	DRAFT in feet
332	291.3	39.2	18.4

GROSS TON	NET TON	TYM	DISP
1823	887	2184	2400

POWER: BOILER   ENGINE
         2 Scotch   *2 TE 23 × 36 × 55/36 each*

BHP (TOTAL)	SPEED (KNOTS)
4500 IHP	*17*

OWNERS:
W. K. Vanderbilt 1893–1910
Ocean Transport Ltd. and Lord Pirrie 1911–1925
British Navy World War I

Valiant was ordered to replace *Alva*, which sank after a collision in 1892. She was one of the most elaborately furnished yachts ever built. Rumor has it that about that time Consuelo Vanderbilt became engaged to the Duke of Marlborough, whom she later married. Her father wished to show the English nobility, who may have had lingering doubts on the marriage of an American into their circle, that he could and did own a yacht superior to any owned by them. A brief summary of her interior furnishings has been given already. She was for many years the largest privately owned yacht afloat, when measured by Thames tonnage, and was as comfortable as she was luxurious. She was one of the first with twin screws. . About 1910 her yards and sails were removed, a spike bowsprit and pole masts replaced her heavy gear, and a raised forecastle and wheelhouse were installed. She served her two owners for nearly 30 years until she was scrapped in 1926.

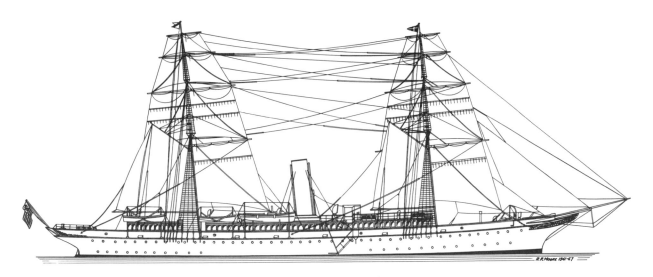

VENETIA ~ 1893

Other Names
SYBARITE
CHEROKEE
NORTH STAR

DESIGNER: *W. C. Storey*

BUILT: *1893* By *Naval Const.*
                    & Arm., Ltd. (later Vickers)

MATERIAL: *Steel*   RIG: *Screw Schooner*

LOA	LWL	BEAM	DRAFT in feet
256	219.5	29.3	16.9

GROSS TON	NET TON	TYM	DISP
819	329	924	

POWER: BOILER   ENGINE
            2 Scotch   *1 TE 21½ × 34 × 56/34*

BHP (TOTAL)   SPEED (KNOTS)
    1115

OWNERS:
Lord Ashburton 1893–1898
Whittaker Wright 1898–1902 (Sybarite)
William Clark 1902 (Cherokee)
Cornelius Vanderbilt 1902–1914 (North Star)
British Navy World War I

84

This *Venetia* was the first of three steam yachts by that name. She was probably best known when she was *North Star*. Her then owner, Gen. Cornelius Vanderbilt, was an experienced yachtsman, in both sail and steam. During his ownership *North Star* served as flagship of the New York Yacht Club and cruised abroad extensively. She was at Cowes when World War I broke out, so she was turned over to the British Navy, serving as a hospital ship. As with so many other yachts, a reconversion to a yacht after service in World War I would have been too costly. She was dropped from Lloyd's listing in 1920.

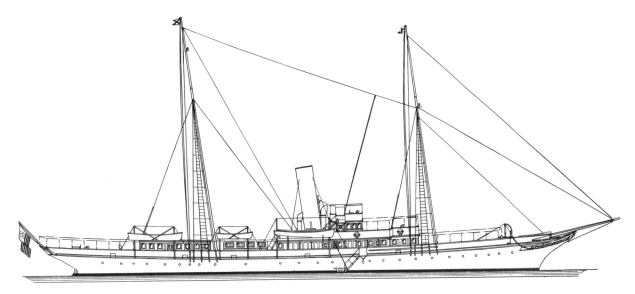

ELEANOR ~ 1894

Other Names
WACOUTA
HARVARD
ATHINIA

DESIGNER: *Charles Hanscom*
BUILT: *1894* By *Bath Iron Works*
MATERIAL: *Steel*   RIG: *Screw Bark*

LOA	LWL	BEAM	DRAFT in feet
243	*208*	*32*	*13.4*

GROSS TON	NET TON	TYM	DISP
803	*402*	*1024*	

POWER: BOILER   ENGINE
       2 Scotch   *1 TE 18 × 28 × 45/30*

BHP (TOTAL)	SPEED (KNOTS)
1000	*14.5*

OWNERS:
W. A. Slater 1894–1899
Mrs. James Martinez-Cardeza 1900
James J. Hill 1901–1916 (Wacouta)
George F. Baker, Jr., 1917 (Harvard)
UN Navy World War I
Commercial Service

Eleanor was the first big yacht built at Bath, and was designed by Charles Hanscom, the yard's naval architect. She served her first two owners well. As the United States was approaching World War I, Mr. Baker offered his yacht *Viking* to the navy. She was not accepted because her bunker capacity was considered too small, so Mr. Baker bought *Eleanor*, changed her name to *Harvard*, and gave her to the Navy. She served on the Breton Patrol during the war. After the war commercial interests in Europe bought her and it is believed that she was still in service in Greek waters as late as 1948.

GIRALDA ~ 1894

DESIGNER: *Cox & King and Fairfield*
BUILT: *1894   By Fairfield SB Co.*
MATERIAL: *Steel*   RIG: *Twin Screw Schooner*

LOA	LWL	BEAM	DRAFT in feet
306	271	35.2	18.0

GROSS TON	NET TON	TYM	DISP
1265		1506	

POWER: BOILER   ENGINE
          5 Scotch   2 TE 25 × 40 × 45 × 45/27 each

BHP (TOTAL):   SPEED (KNOTS):
    7400 IHP   *22.5*

OWNERS:
Col. Harry MacCalmont 1894–1898
Spanish Navy 1898–1935

Giralda was built for Col. Harry MacCalmont, who had inherited a great fortune from an uncle. He became a great horseman and yachtsman, and later built *Banshee* and *Tarantula*. She was bought by the Spanish Navy as a dispatch vessel at the time of the war with the United States. After that brief war she was fitted out and became the Royal Yacht. She was a frequent visitor to Cowes and other English yachting ports as King Alfonso XIII was an ardent meter class racing helmsman. *Giralda* was one of the first yachts to exceed 1000 tons and became a pattern followed by Cox & King in many other yachts; low freeboard, elliptical stern, and tall stack with top parallel to the waterline. Sometime after World War I, in which of course she did not serve, she was listed as a dispatch boat (aviso), and from 1922 to 1935 she was shown in Jane's as in the hydrographic service. She was dropped from Jane's after 1935.

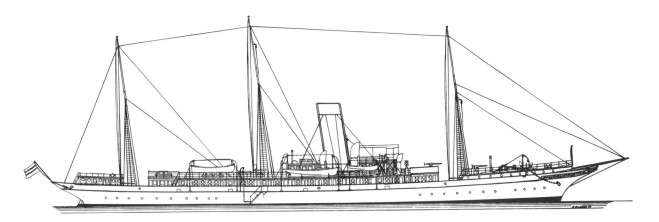

STANDART ~ 1895

Other Names
MARTI

DESIGNER: *Burmeister & Wain*
BUILT: 1895   By *Burmeister & Wain, Copenhagen*
MATERIAL: *Steel*   RIG: *Twin Screw Schooner*

LOA	LWL	BEAM	DRAFT in feet
420	370	50.4	20.0

GROSS TON	NET TON	TYM	DISP
		4334	5980

POWER: BOILER   ENGINE
    4 Water-tube   2 TE 41 × 65 × 105/54 each
    (Oil in 1937)   2 Geared Turbines in 1937

BHP (TOTAL)	SPEED (KNOTS)
10600 IHP	18
11500 BHP	

OWNERS:
Russian Navy 1895–1917 as Royal Yacht
   1917–1963 (Marti)

Standart was the principal royal yacht until the abdication of the Czar around 1917. In the pre-World War I days she was a frequent visitor to Cowes.

After the Revolution she became a mine layer in the Russian Navy. In 1937 she was completely overhauled and rebuilt in Leningrad, with new engines installed. She remained in service as such until at least 1963 when she was dropped from Jane's.

VEGLIA ~ 1895

Other Names
ALCEDO

DESIGNER: *G. L. Watson*
BUILT: *1895* By *D. & W. Henderson*
MATERIAL: *Steel*   RIG: *Screw Barkentine*

LOA	LWL	BEAM	DRAFT in feet
275	*238*	*31*	*16.3*

GROSS TON	NET TON	TYM	DISP
960	*399*	*1111*	

POWER: BOILER   ENGINE
        1 Scotch   *1 TE 23 × 38 ×64/36*
BHP (TOTAL)   SPEED (KNOTS)

OWNERS:
Baron Nathaniel de Rothschild 1895–1905
G. W. C. Drexel 1906–1917
US Navy World War I

92

Veglia was one of several large steam yachts owned by members of the Rothschild banking families. Later, Mr. Drexel of Philadelphia had her for several years before turning her over to the Navy for war service. She was one of a group of yachts that operated out of Brest and other Breton ports on convoy protection. One November night in 1917, a submarine was sighted 300 yards away with torpedo tracks coming toward her. Trying to swing parallel to the tracks, *Alcedo* was struck forward and sank rapidly.

AEGUSA ~ 1896

Other Names
ERIN

DESIGNER: *Scott SB & Eng., Ltd.*
BUILT: *1896   By Scott SB & Eng., Ltd.*
MATERIAL: *Steel*   RIG: *Screw Schooner*

LOA	LWL	BEAM	DRAFT in feet
287	252	31.8	13.0

GROSS TON	NET TON	TYM	DISP
1057	490	1330	

POWER: BOILER   ENGINE
          2 Scotch   *1 TE 24 × 40 × 45 × 45/39*
BHP (TOTAL)   SPEED (KNOTS)

OWNERS:
I. Florio 1896–1897
Sir Thomas Lipton 1898–1914 (Erin)
British Navy World War I (Aegusa)

Although built as *Aegusa,* she was best known as Sir Thomas Lipton's *Erin,* and was of course intimately connected with her owner's quest for the America's Cup with his sailing yachts *Shamrock.* Her arrival in New York in 1899 with the first *Shamrock* coincided with that of Admiral Dewey's on his *Olympia* after his victory at Manila Bay. Lipton had sent a package of tea to each man on the *Olympia* when she stopped at Ceylon en route to the United States, so *Erin* was greeted by Dewey, the hero of the moment. Lipton became a guest of New York City during the Dewey celebrations. On Lipton's return to England after his glorious defeat, he was taken up by the circle around Edward VII, then Prince of Wales. *Erin* was used extensively to entertain this group. By the time *Erin* went to the United States with *Shamrock II,* the parties and people on board *Erin* made her the most sought-after yacht in the United States. She had been decorated in true Victorian fashion, full of bric-a-brac, statuary, ormolu, china cabinets, Sèvres vases, brasses and bronzes,

canaries and all. The same round of parties occurred during the *Shamrock III* series. President Roosevelt had Lipton to lunch at the White House and followed one of the races from *Erin.*

In 1914, *Erin* was en route to the United States with *Shamrock IV,* when war was declared. She took *Shamrock IV* to Bermuda and later to Brooklyn. She was outfitted as a hospital ship and returned to England. She left with Sir Thomas Lipton aboard for what is now Yugoslavia to set up a hospital for the Serbs and Montenegrans, stopping at Monte Carlo and Patras, Greece, en route, where the familiar parties were given aboard. On arrival her staff helped stop a typhus epidemic. *Erin* then returned to England where Sir Thomas gave her to the Admiralty. As there was a battleship *Erin* she took her old name during the war. She served as a hospital ship until torpedoed and sunk in the Mediterranean in June, 1915.

After the War the yacht *Albion* was bought by Lipton and renamed *Erin.*

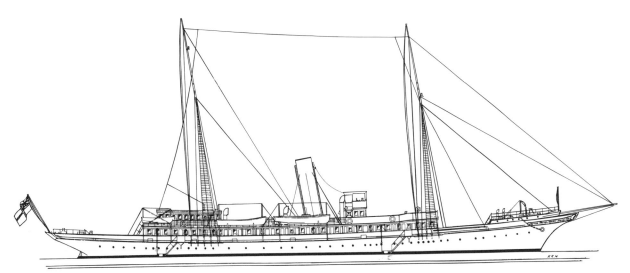

MARGARITA ~ 1896

Other Names
ALBERTA
ROZSVIET
SURPRISE

DESIGNER: *G. L. Watson*
BUILT: *1896 By Ailsa SB Co.*
MATERIAL: *Steel*   RIG: *Twin Screw Schooner*

LOA	LWL	BEAM	DRAFT in feet
278	233	33.5	15.4

GROSS TON	NET TON	TYM	DISP
1144	446	1322	

POWER: BOILER   ENGINE
   2 Scotch (Oil in 1924)   *2 QE 15½ × 22 ×*
                          31 × 44/27 each

BHP (TOTAL)   SPEED (KNOTS)
                           17

OWNERS:
A. J. Drexel 1896–1898
Little & Johnson 1899–1912 (Alberta)
  (King of Belgians 1900–1909)
J. D. Cohn 1912–1914
F. G. Bourne 1915–1917
Russian Navy 1918 (Rozsviet)
British Navy World Wars I and II
  (HMS Surprise, Flagship Mediterranean Fleet)
Not listed 1920–1928
G. H. Williams 1928–1929
Colonial Land & Invest. Ltd. 1930–1933
J. A. MacCandlish 1934–1937
Axa Investment, Ltd. 1939–1950

96

Margarita was one of three yachts by that name, all of which were quite well known as sturdy ocean-going vessels, and all of which had long honorable careers each extending over 30 years.

At some time, I believe it to have been between 1900 and 1909, she was apparently owned by the King of the Belgians, yet neither his name nor that of any Belgian entity is shown in Lloyd's then or during the 1920–1928 era when she was not listed in Lloyd's. Possibly Little & Johnson may have managed her for the King. A plan of her arrangement is shown in Fig. 4.

Again she was reported to have been lost by fire at Lagos in February, 1942, yet she reappears in Lloyd's and was listed as a yacht until 1950.

Of the other two *Margaritas*, one (1889) was originally named *Semiramis*, while the other (1900) was later called *Semiramis*, fine examples of how yachts' names and identities can be confused.

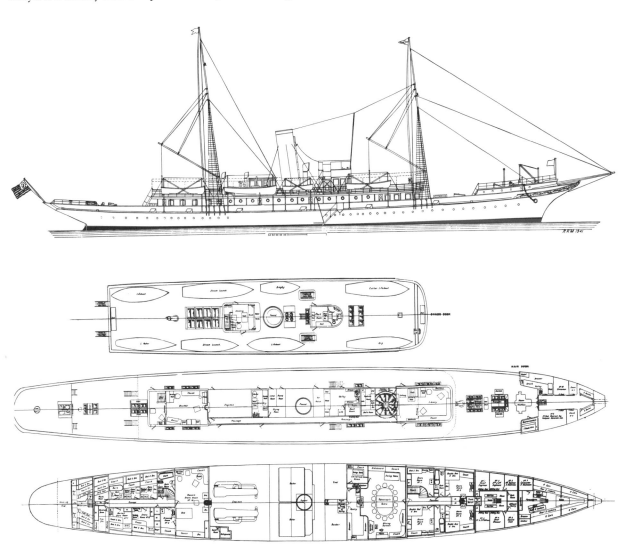

SOVEREIGN ~ 1896

Other Names
USS SCORPION

DESIGNER: *J. Beavor-Webb*
BUILT: *1896 By J. N. Robins, Brooklyn*
MATERIAL: *Steel* RIG: *Twin Screw Schooner*

LOA	LWL	BEAM	DRAFT in feet
250.5	210.5	28.2	12.0

GROSS TON	NET TON	TYM	DISP
627	427		775

POWER: BOILER   ENGINE
   Water-tube   *2 TE 15 × 24 × 39/21 each*

OWNERS:
M. C. D. Borden 1896–1898
US Navy 1898–1928 (USS Scorpion)

Used for only a short time by Mr. Borden before being sold to the Navy for $300,000, *Sovereign* remained in naval service after the war with Spain. She served in the Caribbean area on Panama survey work and on patrols in areas affected by minor uprisings. In 1908 she went to (then) Constantinople as station ship for the ambassador and others. Most of the major powers maintained station ships there at that time. She went to Messina at the time of the earthquake in 1909, carrying medical supplies and staff, and later during earthquakes in Turkey in 1912 she again provided medical help. She was interned in Constantinople during the later part of World War I, but as the United States had not de-clared war on Turkey she was not seized or molested. After the war she remained there as flagship of the U.S. High Commissioner to Turkey until 1923. After operating in the Eastern Mediterranean until 1927, she returned to the United States, where she was decommissioned and finally sold for scrap in 1929.

The same Mr. Borden eventually replaced her with *Little Sovereign*, a fast commuter built by Herreshoff in 1904, and later had another *Little Sovereign* built in 1909 by Seabury. She was replaced, for reasons explained under her text, by another *Sovereign*, known as the fast *Sovereign* or the four funnel *Sovereign*.

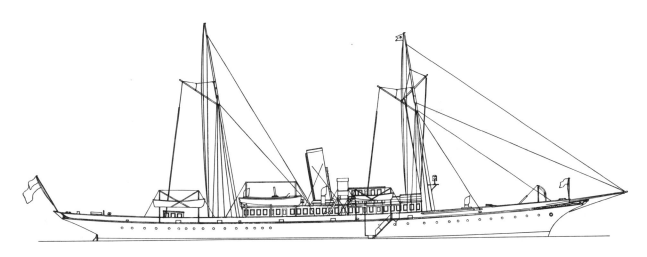

MAYFLOWER ~ 1897

Other Names
MALA
BUTTE

DESIGNER: *G. L. Watson*
BUILT: *1897   By J. & G. Thompson*
MATERIAL: *Steel*   RIG: *Twin Screw Schooner*

LOA	LWL	BEAM	DRAFT in feet
318	*273*	*36.5*	*18.5*

GROSS TON	NET TON	TYM	DISP
1779	*1009*	*1806*	*2690*

POWER: BOILER   ENGINE
        2 Scotch   *2 TE 22½ × 38 × 40 × 40/27*
                         each

BHP (TOTAL)	SPEED (KNOTS)
2400	*16½*

OWNERS:
Ogden Goelet 1897–1898
US Navy, US Coast Guard 1898–1946
Commercial service, Panama flag 1947– (Mala)

Mayflower was one of three very large and luxurious yachts very similar in size and appearance, all designed by Watson and built in 1897. Her owner, Ogden Goelet, whose brother owned the similar *Nahma*, used her for a very short time before he died aboard. She was purchased by the US Navy in 1898, and after being armed, joined the fleet blockading Havana, Cuba, where she engaged shore batteries and captured blockade runners. In 1902 she was recommissioned as the U.S. Presidential Yacht and remained in that service for many years.

Between presidential trips, she was stationed in the Caribbean where she was the scene for the separation of Panama from Colombia. In 1905 Pres. Theodore Roosevelt arranged for the treaty ending the Russo-Japanese War on board her. From the *Mayflower*, President Roosevelt reviewed the "Great White Fleet" on its departure in 1907 and on its return from around the world in 1909. She served on the United States east coast during World War I. President Hoover withdrew her from service as the Presidential Yacht in 1929. She was laid up in the Philadelphia Navy Yard when she was badly burned in June, 1931. The hull was sold to and refitted by H. J. Gielow. The new owner had to sell her, so she went into the South American trade as SS *Butte*. The Maritime Commission acquired her in 1942, and after being refitted and renamed *Mayflower*, she entered the Coast Guard where she served as a training vessel on the east coast of the United States until 1946. The second photograph shows how great a change in appearance can be made, especially under wartime conditions. Decommissioned and sold, she caught fire and was towed to Baltimore. Purchased and put under the Panama flag, she was named *Mala* and carried refugees from France to Israel.

She will always be remembered as the stately U.S. Presidential Yacht.

NAHMA ~ 1897

Other Names
ISTAR

DESIGNER: *G. L. Watson*
BUILT: 1897   By *J. & G. Thompson*
MATERIAL: *Steel*   RIG: *Twin Screw Schooner*

LOA	LWL	BEAM	DRAFT in feet
306	260	36.7	17.5

GROSS TON	NET TON	TYM	DISP
1740	970	1806	

POWER: BOILER   ENGINE
      2 *Scotch*   2 TE 22½ × 38 × 40 × 40/27 *each*

BHP (TOTAL)	SPEED (KNOTS)
2400	16½

OWNERS: *Robert Goelet and Mrs. Goelet 1897–1922*
US Navy World War I
Jeremiah Brown 1923
George E. Millner 1924–1925
C.L. Kerr and R. Thynne 1926–1927

Nahma was built for Robert Goelet, brother of Ogden Goelet who had the near-sister *Mayflower* built at the same time. The Goelet family are property owners in New York City. Her owner used *Nahma* in European waters until World War I. After war service in the Mediterranean she was bought and put under the British flag as *Istar* and operated as a supply vessel on "Rum Row" off the Virginia Capes. In a few voyages she netted her owners close to a million dollars before they wisely retired.

Later on she became a shark oil factory ship, a rather sad ending to a fine yacht. She was broken up about 1936.

TURBINIA ~ 1897

DESIGNER: *Sir Charles Parsons*

BUILT: *1894* BY *C. A. Parsons and Brown &*
1897 *Wood*

MATERIAL: *Steel*   RIG: *Triple Screw Steamer*

LOA   LWL   BEAM   DRAFT in feet
103.3   *100*   *9.0*   *3.0*

GROSS TON   NET TON   TYM   DISP
                                 39   *44½*

POWER: BOILER   ENGINE
        1 Yarrow Water-tube   *1 (1894) then*
                                 3 Turbines (1897)

BHP (TOTAL)   SPEED (KNOTS)
   2000 (3 turb)   *35*

OWNERS:

Marine Steam Turbine Co., Ltd. (Parsons) 1894–1908
Museums in London and Newcastle on Tyne to date

Turbinia was designed by Sir Charles Parsons, inventor and builder of Parsons turbines. She was built by him in 1894 to test Parsons turbines in service and to demonstrate the advantages of turbine vs reciprocating engine propulsion. Naturally the fastest type of craft should be used for such demonstrations. It was a sad blow when, powered by one radial flow turbine, *Turbinia* made less than 20 knots due to cavitation at the high turbine speeds of 1800–2000 RPM. Parsons made many studies of cavitation. The single turbine was removed and replaced by three Parsons parallel-flow turbines, each driving a shaft with three propellers on each shaft.

The Royal Naval Review for Queen Victoria's Jubilee took place at the Spithead in 1897. With all the ships of the Navy, guest vessels, and huge crowds looking on, the tiny (comparatively) *Turbinia* went down the rows of naval vessels at 35 knots. This effectively demonstrated the power and performance of steam turbines, a previously unknown type of high-speed marine power, from a practical point of view. In a very short time successful turbine installations had been made and put in service on coastal steamers. The Cunard Line experimented with turbines in the 20,000 ton *Carmania*, and then entrusted turbines to their *Mauretania* and *Lusitania*. Both ships became world famous, the former holding the transatlantic speed record from 1910 to 1929.

Turbinia was solely a demonstration vessel to show, as she certainly did, the advantages of turbine drive. Her weight of 44½ tons divided by her horsepower gave a very low 49 pounds per horsepower, only to be surpassed five years later by the American *Arrow* which, even with reciprocating engines, achieved a figure of 36 pounds per horsepower.

Turbinia had very little accommodation of any kind as she was designed solely for demonstration. Shortly after being photographed alongside the *Mauretania*, the first large, fast, turbine powered ocean liner, she was laid up on the Tyne. Her after part was retired to exhibition in 1927 in the Imperial Science Museum in London. In 1961 both halves were rejoined in Newcastle on Tyne where she can now be seen.

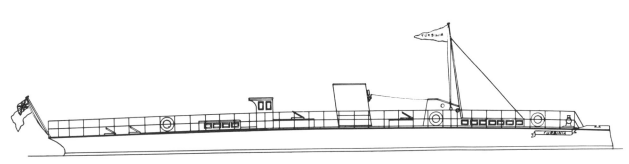

TUSCARORA ~ 1897

Other Names
GOIZEKO IZARRA
ANATOLI

DESIGNER: *G. L. Watson*
BUILT: *1897* BY *Scott SB & Eng. Co.*
MATERIAL: *Steel* RIG: *Screw Schooner*

LOA	LWL	BEAM	DRAFT in feet
204	170	26.8	12.5

GROSS TON	NET TON	TYM	DISP
541	303	591	

POWER: BOILER ENGINE
    1 Scotch   *1 TE 16 × 26 × 41/27*
BHP (TOTAL)   SPEED (KNOTS)

OWNERS:
Mrs. E. B. Laidlaw 1897–1901
Mr. Walter & Mrs. O. B. Jennings 1902–1910
Ramon de la Sota 1911–1922 (Goizeko Izarra)
Godfrey H. Williams 1923 (Tuscarora)
Lord Queenborough 1924–1928
W. G. Macbeth 1929–1936
John Urquhart 1937–1939
British Navy World War II
Commercial interests (Panama) 1947 (Anatoli)

Tuscarora was a typical comfortable Watson yacht lasting well over 40 years as a yacht. She differed from most in that her deckhouse amidships extended the full width of the vessel, eliminating the more commonly seen side decks. She had many owners, but her frequent changes of ownership were not due to any dissatisfaction. After all, she remained a yacht for half a century before entering into commercial service. She was often called "the ladies' yacht" as her first two owners were ladies.

VARUNA ~ 1897

DESIGNER: *G. L. Watson*
BUILT: *1897*   BY *A. & J. Inglis*
MATERIAL: *Steel*   RIG: *Twin Screw Schooner*

OWNERS:
Eugene Higgins 1897–1909

LOA	LWL	BEAM	DRAFT in feet
300	*260*	*35.3*	*17.3*

GROSS TON	NET TON	TYM	DISP
1573	*595*	*1564*	

POWER: BOILER   ENGINE
     2 Scotch   *2 TE 22½ × 38 × 40 × 40/27*
                          each

BHP (TOTAL)   SPEED (KNOTS)
  2400   *16½*

Varuna was the third of the three similar Watson yachts of 1897, the others being *Mayflower* and *Nahma* owned by the Goelet brothers.

Unfortunately *Varuna* was wrecked in the Azores in 1909. Her owner lived most of the time in Europe so she was not as well known in the United States as were her sisters.

There has always been some confusion in distinguishing them. Naturally *Mayflower* changed considerably while she was the U.S. Presidential Yacht, and as mentioned before, she was changed beyond all previous recognition during World War II. However, in their earlier days the following differences might help to identify each one;

Nahma: Yards on foremast, pole masts, two continuous rows of ports forward but no high forecastle with its row of ports.

Mayflower: Yards on foremast, fidded topmasts, two continuous rows of ports on upper main deck including forecastle. This deck plating extended well aft of mainmast.

Varuna: No yards, pole masts with crow's nest on foremast, two continuous rows of ports on upper main deck including forecastle. This deck plating ended at mainmast and continued aft as a deckhouse with side decks.

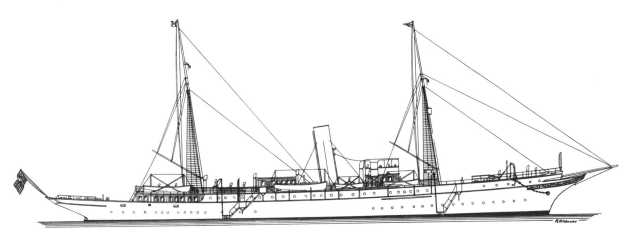

AMERICAN ~ 1898

DESIGNER: *Archibald Watt*
BUILT: *1898*   BY *Archibald Watt*
MATERIAL: *Steel*   RIG: *Screw 3 Masted Ship*

LOA	LWL	BEAM	DRAFT in feet
254	*204*	*34.3*	*14.0*

GROSS TON	NET TON	TYM	DISP
851	*578*	*1140*	

POWER: BOILER   ENGINE
   1 Water-tube   *1 (A Watt) QE 15 ×*
   4 Water-tube in 1907   *21 × 27 × 33/15*
                     1   TE   19 × 30 ×45/
                        26 in 1907

OWNERS:
Archibald Watt 1898–1906
Miss Grace Watt 1907–1911
Haitian Government 1913–1915 (Ferrier)
Commercial interests (oil barge) 1917–1922

I believe that *American* was the only full ship rigged yacht built in the United States. She was also unique in that she was designed by, built by, engined by, and owned by the same man. According to Jane's she became the Haitian Presidential Yacht for two years.

APHRODITE ~ 1898

DESIGNER: *Chas. Hanscom*
BUILT: *1898* BY *Bath Iron Works*
MATERIAL: *Steel*   RIG: *Screw Bark*

LOA	LWL	BEAM	DRAFT in feet
302.6	*260*	*35.6*	*16.0*

GROSS TON	NET TON	TYM	DISP
1148	*654*	*1529*	*1823*

POWER: BOILER   ENGINE
   4 Scotch   *1 TE 28 × 43 × 70/36*

BHP (TOTAL)   SPEED (KNOTS)
   3200   *15*

OWNERS:
Oliver H. Payne 1898–1917
US Navy World War I
Harry Payne Whitney 1919–1928
Commercial interests in Greece 1928–

Aphrodite was Bath designed and Bath built. One of the largest yachts built in the United States, she was a successful and comfortable ocean-going vessel. Her first owner had her for 19 years until he turned her over to the Navy. She, with *Corsair, Noma,* and *Kanahwa*, comprised the group of yachts of the Breton Patrol whose range and sea-keeping abilities permitted their use on extended operations. Around 1910 her yards and sails were removed and her pole mast substituted for the fidded ones.

After the war her second owner kept her in service until she was sold to commercial interests in Greece.

PAYNE YACHT APHRODITE, BUILDING BY THE BATH IRON WORKS, AND DESIGNED BY GENERAL SUPERINTENDENT CHAS. HANSCOM OF THAT INSTITUTION.

ATMAH ~ 1898

DESIGNER: *G. L. Watson*
BUILT: *1898* By *Fairfield SB & Eng., Ltd.*
MATERIAL: *Steel*   RIG: *Twin Screw Schooner*

LOA	LWL	BEAM	DRAFT in feet
°333	300.7	34.3	19.1

GROSS TON	NET TON	TYM	DISP
1665	410	1746	

POWER: BOILER   ENGINE
    3 Scotch   2 TE 20½ × 34 × 37 × 37/27 each

BHP (TOTAL)   SPEED (KNOTS)
                        15.75

OWNERS:
Baron Edmond and J. A. Rothschild 1898–1939
British Navy World Wars I and II

° Supposedly lengthened 30′ in 1901.

Atmah was a typical large seaworthy Watson yacht differing only in her elliptical rather than transom stern. She was owned her entire yachting life by one branch of the Rothschild banking family. She served in both wars, and in World War II was both an anti-aircraft and an accommodation ship.

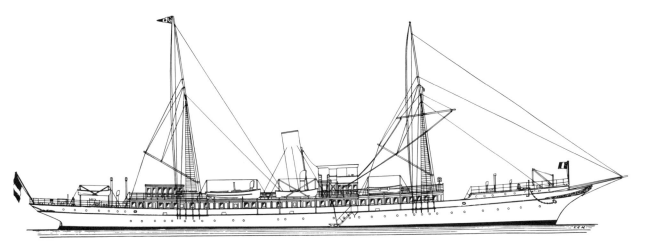

NIAGARA ~ 1898

DESIGNER: *W. G. Shackford*
BUILT: *1898* BY *Harlan & Hollingsworth*
MATERIAL: *Steel* RIG. *Twin Screw Bark*

LOA	LWL	BEAM	DRAFT in feet
272	*247.5*	*36.0*	*18.0*

GROSS TON	NET TON	TYM	DISP
1448	*703*	*1441*	*2600*

POWER: BOILER ENGINE
3 Scotch *2 TE 18 × 28 × 45/30 each*

BHP (TOTAL)	SPEED (KNOTS)
1950	*14*

OWNERS:
Howard Gould 1898–1917
US Navy World War I and to 1939

Niagara was bark-rigged and built in the United States in Wilmington, Delaware by the then well known yard of Harlan & Hollingsworth. She was most elaborately fitted out. The photograph of the staircase in her library (Fig. 2) gives some idea of the opulence of yachts of that era. She was rather unique in that her crew's quarters were aft. She was one of the first vessels fitted with the Londberg stern in which the shaft is enclosed and wide spectacle frames are used in place of shaft brackets. The US Navy made speed trials with the shafts rotating inward and outward. With the outturning shafts she made 14.12 knots at 1950 indicated horsepower, while with inturning screws she made only 12.8 knots even though the indicated power was 2100 horsepower. It was believed that the flow of water being split by the shaft tubing caused the difference in speeds.

After World War I *Niagara* remained in naval service on hydrographic work, mainly in the Caribbean, until 1939. While in naval service her yards, sails, and mizzen mast were removed and the mainmast was relocated aft of her deckhouse.

SURF ~ 1898

DESIGNER: *Cox & King*

BUILT: *1898* BY *Ramage & Ferguson*

MATERIAL: *Steel* RIG: *Screw Schooner*

LOA	LWL	BEAM	DRAFT in feet
200	*166.5*	*24.7*	*13.0*

GROSS TON	NET TON	TYM	DISP
397	*270*	*494*	

POWER: BOILER   ENGINE

2 Scotch   *1 TE 15 × 24 × 39/27*

BHP (TOTAL)   SPEED (KNOTS)

OWNERS:

F. D. Lambert 1898–1900

C. K. G. Billings 1901–1908

J. H. Hanan 1909–1916

J. A. Harriss 1917–1923

Leo Shinasi 1923–1927

John F. Daniell 1928–1929

F. deL. Brown 1930–1931

Margaree SS Co. (W. N. MacDonald) 1933–1950

Surf spent most of her life under United States ownership. During Prohibition she became a rum-runner. On June 14, 1931 a patrolling Coast Guard destroyer (commanded, by the way, by Lieutenant Commander Stone, pilot of the NC 4, the first plane to cross the Atlantic) noticed a splendid white steam yacht flying the burgee of the New York Yacht Club. She was coasting along the Long Island shore, with her owner and guests lounging on deck in yachtsmen's clothes. A careful observation noted that the portholes were covered by plates and the owner's party had extremely dirty hands. So she was stopped, boarded, and found to have over 4000 cases of liquor aboard. She was dropped from Lloyd's after 1950, having spent her latter years under Canadian registry.

There was another *Surf*, also designed by Cox & King, similar in size to this one, but built by Hawthorne in 1902. She was about 550 TYM. Her life as a yacht was under British registry. She went into commercial service in 1950.

CORSAIR (3rd) ~ 1899

Other Names
USS OCEANOGRAPHER

DESIGNER: *J. Beavor-Webb*
BUILT: *1899   BY T. S. Marvel, Newburgh, New York*
MATERIAL: *Steel*   RIG: *Twin Screw Schooner*

LOA	LWL	BEAM	DRAFT in feet
304	*254*	*33.5*	*16.0*

GROSS TON	NET TON	TYM	DISP
1136	*772*	*1396*	

POWER: BOILER   ENGINE
   2 Water-tube   *2 TE*
   (Oil in 1923)   21 × 33 × 38 × 38/30 each

BHP (TOTAL)	SPEED (KNOTS)
6000 IHP	*19*

OWNERS:
J. Pierpont Morgan, J. P. Morgan 1899–1930
US Navy 1917–1919, 1942–1944
U.S. Coast & Geodetic Survey 1930–1942
   (Oceanographer)

120

If any yacht deserves the title of "THE Steam Yacht" it is this beautifully proportioned, handsome, fast, seaworthy vessel. She was designed by that master of graceful line J. Beavor-Webb and built by T. S. Marvel with the finest job of plating known. Only the plating of *Isis* by the same designer and builder could match *Corsair*. This *Corsair* was the third one of that name owned by J. Pierpont Morgan and, after his death, by his son. He had turned over his second *Corsair* to the Navy in 1898. This *Corsair* was about 60′ longer than the second. More powerful and faster than her predecessor, she differed principally in that she was twin screw, to provide better turning ability particularly in the Hudson River near her owner's home. Other than these differences, her owner specified that she should be the same as the second *Corsair* in every way. She was commissioned in 1899, and as her owner was Commodore of the New York Yacht Club at the time, she immediately became the Club's flagship.

Throughout her life she was always the outstanding yacht in any group. The beautiful sheer of her shining black hull, her gilded figurehead and trailboards, the superb shape of her clipper bow (a most difficult line to achieve beauty at all angles), her perfectly raked tall masts, and perfectly proportioned funnel, made her the ideal of a yacht, majestic as well as graceful from any angle. She was beautifully maintained. Her captain during all or nearly all her life, as well as captain of the fourth *Corsair*, was W. B. Porter, a ship's officer whom Mr. Morgan obtained from one of the lines of his International Mercantile Marine. Captain Porter was able to select his own officers and crew, so there was little turnover in *Corsair's* complement.

The forward and after deckhouses were lounging rooms. The companion from the forward deckhouse led below to the dining room, which, located on the berth deck, had a dome over it extending to the main deck between the deckhouses. The companion from the after deckhouse led below to six large staterooms, a large library, and cabins for maids and valets. Curiously, there was no enclosed passageway for the owner and guests to go from their quarters aft to the dining room without going on deck.

The crew's quarters were forward of the dining room. The central or main deckhouse housed the galley, two staterooms, (chief engineer and radio room), the boiler uptakes, and the engine room fidley. The cylinders of the engines in view through the deckhouse, were lagged in polished maple panelling while, of course, the metal parts of the engines were highly polished or brightly painted.

Her owner used her extensively, not only in summers as a floating home near New York, but for commuting to and from his estate on the Hudson River. He also used her often as a place for business meetings, where he and his guests could enjoy privacy and lack of distraction. Mr. Morgan made many trips to Europe, where he had a town house and a country place in England and frequented the Bristol Hotel in Paris and the Grand Hotel in Rome. At least six times (1902, 1905, 1907, 1909, 1911, 1912) he sent *Corsair* ahead to Europe while he travelled over on one of the White Star liners of the International Mercantile Marine. *Corsair* made trips in the North Sea, the Mediterranean, and British waters on those occasions. He would be at Cowes during Cowes week, at Kiel during Kiel week, and on at least one such occasion he was guest of the Kaiser. Royalty and the great of many nations were graciously entertained on *Corsair*. Wherever she went, the beautiful *Corsair* stood out among all other yachts even though they might be bigger. Mr. Morgan would usually send *Corsair* back to the United States while he completed his visits to London, Paris, Rome, and other places where he collected articles for his great collection of art. On his return on a White Star liner, it was a matter of pride for *Corsair* to meet the liner outside New York harbor and escort her in.

After J. Pierpont Morgan's death in 1913, his son J. P. Morgan, Jr. inherited *Corsair* and devoted as much time and love to her as did his father. J. P. Morgan lived at Matinicock Pt. on the shore of Long Island, so *Corsair* moored at Glen Cove, Long Island instead of up the Hudson River.

Due to the war her new owner could not take her to Europe. When the United States declared war, he turned *Corsair* over to the Navy. She was converted to accommodate 134 officers and men, instead of her normal complement of 55. Guns, depth charges, ammunition storage were fitted, her bowsprit was removed, and a wheelhouse was installed. When she sailed, painted a dull gray, she was hardly recognizable as the *Corsair* of yore. Initially the Navy required a regular Naval officer to be in command. Lt. Comdr. T. A. Kittinger filled that post. Her executive officer was her peacetime skipper, W. B. Porter. What could have been a difficult relationship never occurred because of the characters of both men. Captain Porter was often referred to as "Skipper" (not the skipper), and on at least one occasion, when picking up life boats and rafts from the sunken *Antilles* in a heavy sea, Commander Kittinger told "Skipper" to take her. After some months Commander Kittinger was promoted and Lieutenant Commander Porter again commanded *Corsair* for the rest of the war. Her peacetime chief engineer, chief officer, and several of her crew started out in USS *Corsair* as part of a crew that included many Princeton men. Eighteen including Commander Porter and Lieutenant McGuire served only on her during her naval service.

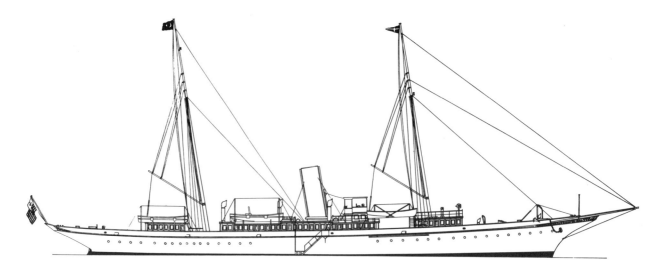

Corsair sailed from New York on June 14, 1917, and formed part of the Breton Patrol operating on convoy work out of Brest, St. Nazaire, and other ports. She, together with Aphrodite, Noma, and Kanahwa, being the largest and most seaworthy of the Breton Patrol yachts, operated farther to sea than did the others. Corsair served on this duty until the Armistice. One October night in 1917 she sighted and tried to ram and depth charge the German U-60 but without success. During this time she steamed over 19,000 miles in five months without shutting down her boilers, a great tribute to her construction and to her peacetime chief engineer and his staff. On December 14, 1917, she stood out as part of a fast (14 knot) convoy. A storm was encountered which developed into that of December 1917, the worst ever known to Breton fishermen. Corsair hung on as long as possible until, unable to return to Brest, she ran before it at 5 knots to reach Lisbon. She was six weeks in the dockyard undergoing repairs during which time Mr. Morgan arranged for a Christmas dinner for all hands. While she was in the dockyard there was a minor revolution and Corsair was hit by some rifle and shell fire, ironically the only time she was subjected to gunfire. In June she stood by and tried to take in tow the mined SS Californian. This stricken ship was the only one lost in convoys protected by Corsair and other yachts. Even then the loss was due to a mine. In September, Corsair towed the disabled steamer Dagfin 300 miles to safety, a splendid piece of seamanship.

After the armistice, she served briefly as Admiral Sims' flagship and performed other duties before returning to the United States for decommissioning and refitting as a yacht again. While in Europe she had steamed 49,984 miles.

During refitting she was fitted with oil-burning water-tube boilers. The forward deckhouse was removed and the main deckhouse was extended forward, over the old dining room dome to the foremast. The new dining room was in the extended deckhouse, forward of the galley, while the old dining space became an enlargement of the crew space. Captain Porter resumed command, and Corsair became again the beautiful yacht she had been before.

Eventually Mr. Morgan ordered a new Corsair (4th), so in 1930 the grand old lady was given to the U.S. Coast & Geodetic Survey. Named Oceanographer, Corsair engaged in survey work offshore, using many new and experimental sonic depth-measuring devices. One of the undersea canyons on the east coast of the United States is named "Oceanographer Canyon." When the United States entered World War II, the Navy asked for her again for urgent survey work in the Pacific. She was fitted out and commissioned in the Navy again. She carried out surveys in the Aleutians, Solomon Islands, and other South Pacific areas until she returned to the United States in August 1944 for a badly needed overhaul. On inspection it was found that too much work would be necessary, with the limited personnel available, to put her in shape again. She was decommissioned on September 21, 1944, and in accordance with Mr. Morgan's conditions was scrapped late in 1944.

Thus after 45 years of service, not only as a yacht but under rigorous service in two wars (when passenger ships and tankers are written off after 20 years), the grandest yacht of all has gone. Corsair was a tribute to her designer J. Beavor-Webb, to T. S. Marvel her builder and W. A. Fletcher her engine builder, to Capt. W. B. Porter her captain, and, above all, to both J. P. Morgans, her devoted owners.

KANAHWA ~ 1899

Other Names
USS PIQUA

DESIGNER: *Charles L. Seabury*
BUILT: *1899* BY *Gas Eng. & Power and C.L.*
                                              Seabury
MATERIAL: *Steel*   RIG: *Twin Screw Schooner*

LOA	LWL	BEAM	DRAFT in feet
227	192	24.3	11.5

GROSS TON	NET TON	TYM	DISP
475	323	583	575

POWER: BOILER   ENGINE
    2 Water-tube   *2 TE 14¼ × 24 × 42/24 each*

BHP (TOTAL)   SPEED (KNOTS)
                          20½

OWNERS:
John P. Duncan 1899–1901
H. H. Rogers 1901–1911
Adram Baudouine 1911–1915
M. F. Plant 1915
John Borden 1916–1917
US Navy World War I (USS Piqua)
John Borden 1919–1920
James Briggs 1920–1921
Commerical interests 1922

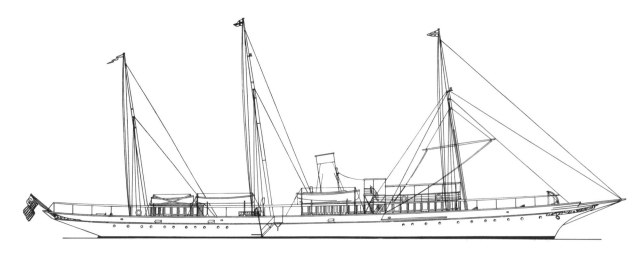

Kanahwa was the fastest of the non-express sea-going yachts of her era, as well as one of the handsomest. She is best known for her two races for the Lysistrata Cup in 1903 and 1904. On July 24, 1903, she raced *Noma* (q.v.). The start was off Brenton's Reef, Newport. Black smoke from soft coal poured from *Noma's* (then single) funnel, while from *Kanahwa's* funnel came only a light brown smoke from the hand-picked hard coal she used for the race. After all, her owner owned the Virginian Railway that hauled coal from the Kanahwa mines. After 15 miles *Kanahwa* was ahead by 1′57″ averaging 19.9 knots. The second 15 miles of the triangular course gave Kanahwa a lead of 4′05″ at a speed of 20.62 knots, after which she slowed slightly to finish 3′56″ ahead of the disappointed *Noma*. On June 18, 1904, she raced *Hauoli* off Sandy Hook on a similar course. *Kanahwa* averaged just over 20 knots to finish 3′29″ ahead. After that race nobody wished to challenge *Kanahwa* for the Lysistrata Cup.

While owned by H. H. Rogers, *Kanahwa* was used mainly between New York and Fairhaven (New Bedford), Massachusetts, where her owner had his summer home. As the route between these ports was almost identical to that followed by the Fall River and New Bedford passenger steamers, Mr. Rogers obtained the services of Capt. E. R. Geer, probably the most skillful (or daring) of that superb group of ship handlers. Rain or fog, clear or stormy, *Kanahwa* ran between these ports on a clock-like schedule, through such treacherous waters as Buzzards Bay, Block Island and Long Island Sounds, and the Race. She bucked heavy traffic, strong tidal currents, and frequent fogs, without any electrical aids to navigation, even radio, but only compass, rev. counters, and foghorn or whistle. The frontispiece shows *Kanahwa* under Captain Geer charging through other steam yachts.

Kanahwa's seaworthiness was amply proven by her service on the Breton Patrol during World War I. She, *Corsair*, *Aphrodite*, and her late competitor, *Noma*, served as the four yachts of the Breton Patrol that operated far out to sea. As the US Navy already had a collier with the name USS *Kanahwa*, the yacht was officially commissioned as USS *Piqua*, though because of her fame and distinctive appearance she was still called *Kanahwa*.

After World War I she returned to her prewar owner. She soon went into commercial service. But after over 20 years of hard, driving yacht service, service in the wintry Bay of Biscay, this lightly built, speedy vessel reached the state where she had to be broken up about 1922.

Thus departed the fastest all-around steam yacht of the era.

~

Scout, the first of this group, was ordered by and built for August Belmont (who represented the Rothschilds in the United States) as a tender to his 70′ racing sloop. So satisfactory was *Scout* that others were built as tenders to powerless sailing yachts or as among the first of the steamers used solely for commuters. Light in weight, reasonably fast (17–18 knots), and, for the uses to which they were put, good sea boats, they filled a need and deservedly lasted for some time.

SCOUT ~ 1899

Other Names
DAWN
MIRAGE
NIAGARA (III)
STROLLER
TRAMP
ZINGANEE
EXPRESS

DESIGNER: *N. G. Herreshoff*
BUILT: *1899* **By** *Herreshoff Mfg. Co.*
MATERIAL: *Wood* **RIG:** *Screw Steamer*

LOA	LWL	BEAM	DRAFT in feet
°81	72	10.5	3.3

GROSS TON	NET TON	TYM	DISP
30	20		

POWER: BOILER   ENGINE
    1 Water-tube   *1 TE 6 × 10 × 16/9*

BHP (TOTAL)	SPEED (KNOTS)
350 est	*18*

OWNERS:

Scout: August Belmont	Built *1899*
Mirage: Cornelius Vanderbilt	*1899*
Niagara: Howard Gould	*1901*
Tramp: W. O. Gray	*1901*
Dawn: J. S. Newberry	*1901*
Stroller: G. T. Rafferty	*1900*
Zinganee: W. H. Moore	*1901*
° Express: M. F. Plant 89' LOA	*1903*

VICTORIA and ALBERT (3rd) ~ 1899

DESIGNER: *Sir William White*
BUILT: *1899* BY *Pembroke Dockyard*
MATERIAL: *Steel with Extra Teak*   RIG: *Twin Screw*
    Planking   *Schooner*
    Copper Bottomed

OWNERS:
British Navy as Royal Yacht

LOA	LWL	BEAM	DRAFT in feet
430	*380*	*50*	*17*

GROSS TON	NET TON	TYM	DISP
		5000	*5500*

POWER: BOILER   ENGINE
   18 Water-tube 2 TE 26½ × 44½ × 53 ×
    (Oil later)   *53/39 each*

BHP (TOTAL)	SPEED (KNOTS)
11800	*20.7*

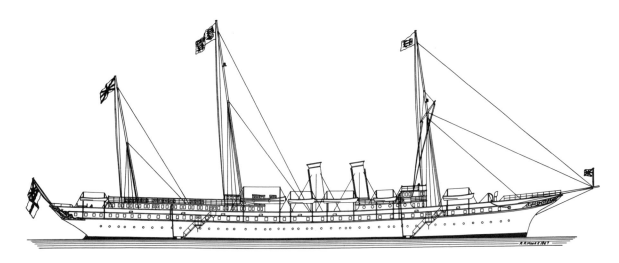

After the previous *Victoria and Albert* had served Queen Victoria for over 40 years it was obvious that, in spite of the Queen's love for her, she had seen her day, and a successor was due. Sir William White, Director of Naval Construction, was entrusted with her design and the supervision of her construction. Unfortunately he was very busy with an extensive naval construction program and apparently did not designate one single person to be the project engineer in full charge of her design and construction.

The design was started. Curiously, she was a complete steel vessel but had extra teak planking over the steel that was coppered below the waterline, presumably to preserve a more even temperature aboard, to reduce noises, and to present a smoother hull. Many mementoes of the old *Victoria and Albert* had to be incorporated, and additional accommodations were desired. Various people insisted on additional fittings, furnishings, and decorations, most of which were high up in the vessel. It is always difficult to reject the requests of an owner, especially if the owner is the Sovereign.

She was launched successfully and put in drydock for the installation of her machinery and all her fittings and furnishings. Finally the dock was flooded to float her out. Before her stern lifted clear she heeled to starboard, knocking out the shores, and listed to 8°. Slowly the list increased to 24°, but by counterballasting this was reduced to 10°. Although her bottom was dented and she had leaks, she was floated, ballasted to an even keel, and towed to Portsmouth Dockyard for correction. Here she was reconstructed, masts were shortened, top hamper was ruthlessly reduced. It is said that G. L. Watson, with his experience in steam yachts, was called in as a consultant. From a designed metacentric height of 2' in loaded condition and 0.83' light, this had been allowed with an increased weight of 711 tons to be reduced to 3 INCHES loaded and negative light. After reconstruction her metacentric heights were 2.7' loaded and 1½' light, a satisfactory margin. On a voyage to Gibralter, she was allowed to lay broadside, without headway, in a 25 foot sea, thus proving her stability. For the rest of her career she was considered seaworthy, but never beautiful in spite of her length. She was majestic in appearance and became well loved.

She served five monarchs as the Royal Yacht. She made several cruises to the Baltic and Russia as well as several to the Mediterranean. However, for extensive voyages the Royal personages usually chartered a passenger vessel or used a warship such as the *Renown* or *Hood*. None of the last three kings used her extensively. George V would race *Britannia* on those occasions when he could get away. Edward VIII's reign was short, but even then he chartered *Nahlin* for his only cruise, whereas George VI's use was curtailed by the War and post-war problems. However, all used her for Fleet Reviews and for Cowes weeks. The success or failure of Cowes week depended to a great extent on the presence of the *Victoria and Albert*, and her presence at any regatta around the coast would make such an event an historic one.

She was a comfortable vessel on such occasions, and she herself was a veritable museum of maritime lore. Her ornate steering wheel and binnacles had come from the Royal Sailing Yacht *Royal George* of 1814. After serving on all three *Victoria and Alberts* they are now on the Royal Yacht *Britannia*.

The new Royal Yacht *Britannia* was designed in 1951, and when completed in 1954 she replaced the grand old *Victoria and Albert*. After 55 years of service, *Victoria and Albert* was scrapped in 1955.

Throughout World War I the crews of the various Royal Yachts manned the battleship *Agincourt*, remaining together until they returned to the Royal Yachts after the war.

LYSISTRATA ~ 1900

Other Names
YAROSLAVNA
VOROVSKY

DESIGNER: *G. L. Watson*
BUILT: *1900*   By *Wm. Denny & Son*
MATERIAL: *Steel*   RIG: *Twin Screw Steamer*

LOA	LWL	BEAM	DRAFT in feet
314.5	*285.0*	*40.0*	*16.0*

GROSS TON	NET TON	TYM	DISP
1942	*626*	*2089*	

POWER: BOILER   ENGINE
     4 Scotch   *2 TE 23 × 38 × 40 × 40/27 each*

BHP (TOTAL)	SPEED (KNOTS)
3500	*19.3*

OWNERS:
James Gordon Bennett 1911–1914
Russian Navy 1914– (Yaroslavna, Vorovsky)

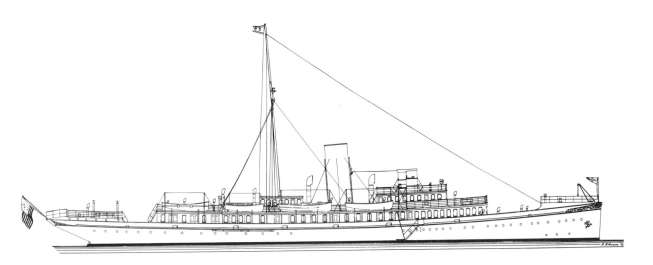

Lysistrata was built for James Gordon Bennett, probably as experienced a seagoing yachtsman in both sail and steam as any at that time. He had owned and raced the schooners *Henrietta* and *Dauntless* across the Atlantic before he had the steamer *Namouna*. *Lysistrata* has often been referred to as the most luxurious, comfortable, and commodious yacht of her time.

Her impulsive owner used her for extravagant entertainment, as well as spur-of-the-moment voyages, until newspaper people on his New York Herald would dread a summons to go aboard *Lysistrata*.

They never knew whether they would receive five minutes of instruction or make a voyage of many days, several weeks or even some months. She must have been exactly what he wanted, because this experienced and impulsive owner kept her for the rest of his life.

She was sold to Russia in World War I as a gunboat until converted to a fishery protection vessel. In the latter guise, she was listed in Jane's up to 1966.

In her day as a yacht, she was the largest privately owned yacht on the basis of gross tonnage, *Valiant* having a larger Thames tonnage.

129

MARGARITA ~ 1900

Other Names
SEMIRAMIS
MLADA
ALACRITY

DESIGNER: *G. L. Watson*
BUILT: *1900* By *Scott SB & Eng. Co., Ltd.*
MATERIAL: *Steel* RIG: *Twin Screw Schooner*

LOA	LWL	BEAM	DRAFT in feet
323	272	36.5	16.8

GROSS TON	NET TON	TYM	DISP
1830	867	1797	

POWER: BOILER ENGINE
  2 Scotch *2 TE 22 × 36 × 40 × 40/27 each*

BHP (TOTAL)	SPEED (KNOTS)
5000	17.0

OWNERS:
A. J. Drexel 1900–1911
Marquis of Anglesey 1912-1913 (Semiramis)
Princess Schahovsky-Gleboff-Strechneff 1914–1924
Russian Navy 1919 (Mlada)
British Navy World War I and II
Cmdr. and Mrs. M. Grahame-White 1924–1939
  (Alacrity)

130

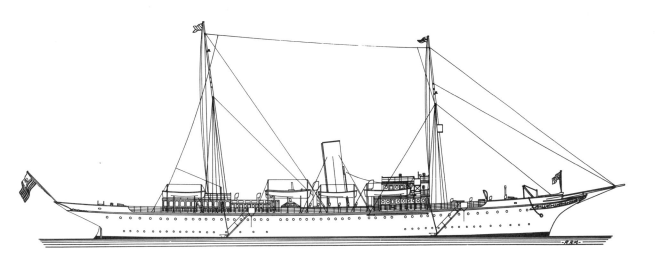

This *Margarita* was the third craft of that name owned by A. J. Drexel, the Philadelphia banker affiliated with the Morgan interests. The others were *Margarita* (1889) and *Margarita* (1896). She was one of the most luxurious of many luxurious yachts of that era. She appears to have been in both the Russian and British Navies in World War I and thereafter. Some years after that war, Montague Grahame-White bought her to form part of his extensive fleet of yachts available for charter. His idea was a good one, but the frightful overhead on yachts not earning their keep eventually forced him out of that business.

In 1925, for example, he had *Alacrity*, as she was then called, available for charter at £40,000 for ten months plus, of course, the expenses of a 60-man crew, food, fuel, expenses, etc. In the 1930's, unable to find a charter, Grahame-White moored her on the south coast of England and rented her accommodations to "trippers" who could "enjoy" the luxury of millionaires for a weekend or so, and be photographed on their "yacht" (for a day). World War II took her over, to the great relief of her owner. She was sunk on active service in the British Navy.

BANSHEE ~ 1901

Other Names
AMELIA
CINCO DU OCTOUBRO

DESIGNER: *Cox and King*
BUILT: *1901* By *Ramage & Ferguson*
MATERIAL: *Steel*   RIG: *Twin Screw Schooner*

LOA	LWL	BEAM	DRAFT in feet
229.5	223.5	29.5	10.5

GROSS TON	NET TON	TYM	DISP
993	310	899	1343

POWER: BOILER   ENGINE
         2 Scotch   *2 TE 16 × 26 × 42/24 each*

OWNERS:
Col. Harry MacCalmont 1901–1905
Portuguese Navy 1905–1908 (Amelia—Royal Yacht)
    1908–1937 (Cinco du Octoubro)

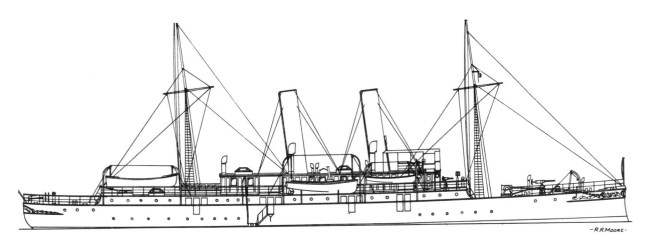

-R.R.Moore-

Banshee was an exception to the usual steam yacht of her era in that she did not have the clipper bow. She was almost naval in appearance. After her first owner died, she became the Portuguese Royal Yacht until the assassination of King Carlos, when she became a dispatch vessel in the Portuguese Navy. She was dropped from Jane's after 1937.

ARROW ~ 1902

DESIGNER: *Charles D. Mosher*
BUILT: *1902   By S. Ayers, Nyack*
MATERIAL: *Comp.—Steel-Aluminum*   RIG:
          Wood Plank   *Twin Screw Str.*

LOA	LWL	BEAM	DRAFT in feet
130	*130*	*12.5*	*3.6*

GROSS TON	NET TON	TYM	DISP
82	*56*		*67*

POWER: BOILER   ENGINE
     2 Water-tube   2 QE 11 × 17 × 24 ×
     (1 removed 1903)   32/15 each
BHP (TOTAL)   SPEED (KNOTS)
     7000   39 (30 on 1 Boiler)

OWNERS:
Charles R. Flint 1902–1906
E. F. Whitney 1907–1914
J. Stuart Blackton 1914–1916
Theodore Krumm 1916–1918
V. S. Briggs 1918–1920

Arrow has always been the subject of great discussion for her speed. She was an express yacht that made one set of measured runs of an average of 45.6 statute miles per hour (or 39 knots). She was built for Charles R. Flint, a well-known entrepreneur of the period. When political fears mounted prior to the Spanish-American War, Mr. Flint ordered two 3500-horsepower steam engines to be installed in a torpedo boat he hoped to sell to the US Navy, which at that time was inferior to the Spanish Navy in torpedo boats. Before the engines were finished the war had ended and the Navy was interested only in destroyers with powers well in excess of the 7000 horsepower that Mr. Flint had on hand. So he had C. D. Mosher design a steam yacht to make a world's record speed using his two engines. *Arrow* was the result. Composite built of steel and aluminum with double mahogany planking, she was unbelievably light for her size. Her weight (displacement) was only 67 tons for a length of 132'. Mosher, a brilliant designer and engineer, gave her a flat run aft, an innovation at that time, so that *Arrow* could absorb the 7000 horsepower without squatting. When announced, her record speed achieved the widest publicity. Her speed was compared to locomotives and to the new automobile. Mr. Flint, entrepreneur that he was, was not averse to such fame. The Russo-Japanese war scare was mounting, so Mr. Flint sent a model of *Arrow*, outfitted as a torpedo boat, to the Grand Duke Alexander Michelo-vitch of Russia. As a result of Flint's and *Arrow's* fame, he was able to sell the Russians munitions, torpedo boats, and submarines at prices that gave him a nice profit above the cost of *Arrow*. Contrary to various stories, *Arrow* herself was not sold to Russia, only a model of her was presented. She served for some years after as a fast commuter but never again tried for record speeds, as her forward boiler was removed. Even so, she made 30 knots thereafter on the one remaining boiler. It was not expected that she would last a long time, with the aluminum in her construction, yet she was dropped from Lloyd's Register as late as 1921 on a life of 18 years.

In comparing *Arrow's* speed with other craft, the French destroyer *Le Terrible* (2569 tons displacement), built in 1933, reached a record of 45.25 knots (53 statute miles per hour) on 100,000 horsepower, and on an 8 hour trial averaged 43 knots. Recently it has been admitted that the passenger liner *United States* made 42 knots during her trials.

A measure of C. D. Mosher's skill as an engineer is demonstrated by *Arrow's* total weight per horsepower of 36 pounds. This, on a vessel with reciprocating engines and some measure of interior accommodations at least sufficient to keep her in service for 18 years, compared favorably to the 49 pounds per horsepower of *Turbinia*, built solely to demonstrate the light weight and power of Parson's turbines.

AZTEC ~ 1902

DESIGNER: *Wm. Gardner*
BUILT: *1902*   By *Lewis Nixon (Crescent SY)*
MATERIAL: *Steel*   RIG: *Twin Screw Schooner*

LOA	LWL	BEAM	DRAFT in feet
263	216	30.0	14.0

GROSS TON	NET TON	TYM	DISP
848	576	890	

POWER: BOILER   ENGINE
   2 Scotch (Oil in 1929)   *2 TE 16 × 25 ×*
                    28½ × 28½/24 each

BHP (TOTAL)   SPEED (KNOTS)
                    15.9

OWNERS:
A. C. Burrage 1902–1940
US Navy World War I
T. H. P. Molsom 1940
Canadian Navy World War II (HMCS Beaver)
W. N. McDonald 1948–1957 (Beaver)

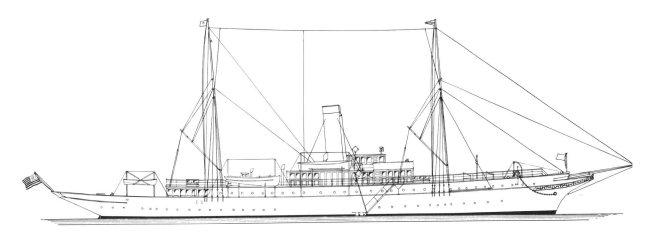

This yacht, eventually christened *Aztec* was, we understand, originally ordered by Henry Clay Pierce, of Mexican oil fame, and was to have been named *Orizaba*. Whether his famous question to J. Pierpont Morgan and the latter's advice on the cost of ownership of yachts were responsible, it is said that he did not accept this yacht and bought a smaller one from Portugal which he named *Yacona*. In any case A. C. Burrage, a Boston copper financier, completed the yacht, which was named *Aztec*. She remained in the Burrage family throughout her career as a yacht up to World War II. She served in both wars, the first in the US Navy and the second in the Canadian Navy. She was dropped from Lloyd's in 1957 after 55 years of service.

Aztec was one of the few pure steam yachts designed by Gardner, who was famous chiefly for beautiful sailing craft such as *Atlantic*, *Sea Call*, and *Vanitie* as well as several P. and R. class boats and many others.

ISIS ~ 1902

DESIGNER: *J. Beavor-Webb*
BUILT: *1902   By T. S. Marvel, Newburgh*
MATERIAL: *Steel*   RIG: *Twin Screw Schooner*

LOA	LWL	BEAM	DRAFT in feet
203	*160*	*24.5*	*11.8*

GROSS TON	NET TON	TYM	DISP
377	*256*	*509*	

POWER: BOILER   ENGINE
      2 Water-tube   2 TE 12 × 18½ × 29/20 each

BHP (TOTAL)	SPEED (KNOTS)
	15

OWNERS:
W. S. and J. T. Spaulding 1902–1915
US Navy World War I
U.S. Coast & Geodetic Survey 1915–1920

Isis was another yacht designed by that master of beauty who was responsible for both *Corsair* (2nd) and *Corsair* (3rd). *Isis* was built at the same yard that built the incomparable *Corsair* (3rd). Both yachts were renowned as having the finest, fairest plating of any vessel. *Isis* was under only one ownership as a yacht. She was well known for having a large pipe organ in her forward deckhouse. During World War I she served in the Navy as a reporting or boarding ship off Ambrose Lightship, New York.

She was sold to the Coast & Geodetic Survey, and put in good service for them. Unfortunately, in searching for a submerged obstruction in the Florida Keys she went aground and became a total loss in February, 1920, a sad end for a superb yacht that had many more years of useful life.

NOMA ~ 1902

DESIGNER: *Tams, Lemoine & Crane*
BUILT: *1902   By Staten Id. SB Co.*
MATERIAL: *Steel*   RIG: *Twin Screw Schooner*

LOA	LWL	BEAM	DRAFT in feet
262	226	28.5	13.5

GROSS TON	NET TON	TYM	DISP
763	519	873	

POWER: BOILER   ENGINE
     4 Water-tube   2 TE 17 × 27 × 32 × 32/24 each

BHP (TOTAL)	SPEED (KNOTS)
4500	19

OWNERS:
W. B. Leeds 1902–1910
J. J. Astor, Vincent Astor 1910–1921
US Navy World War I
Rodman Wanamaker 1921–1926
N. B. Worden 1927–1933
Commercial service 1934

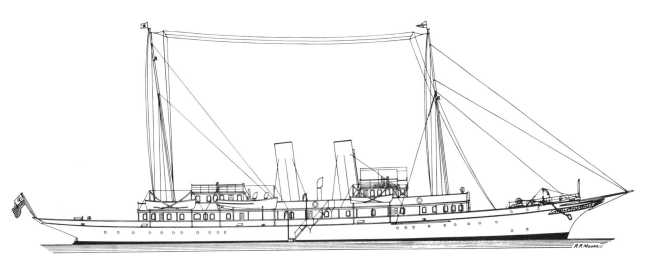

Noma was designed by Clinton Crane, originally to be a sister of *Rheclair*. Her owner and *Rheclair's*, Daniel Reid, had been partners in the tin-plate trust before selling out. Clinton Crane's problems with her owner and the changes involved have been described before in the text. Her designer claimed she was half sunk due to the excessive weights added, yet she put in many years of good service. She was fast, and in 1903 her owner challenged *Kanahwa* for the Lysistrata Cup. *Kanahwa* easily beat *Noma*. *Noma* was changed to a two funnel design about the time she was sold to J. J. Astor and was distinctive thereafter.

She served in the Breton Patrol in World War I, with *Corsair*, *Aphrodite*, and *Kanahwa*. After the war she was laid up for sale for some time before being purchased by Rodman Wanamaker. She eventually went into commercial service under the Italian flag as *Salvator Drimo*. She was dropped from Lloyd's in 1934.

ROAMER ~ 1902

DESIGNER: *N. G. Herreshoff*
BUILT: *1902*   By *Herreshoff Mfg. Co.*
MATERIAL: *Wood*   RIG: *Screw Schooner*

LOA	LWL	BEAM	DRAFT in feet
93.8	82.6	17.2	4.9

GROSS TON	NET TON	TYM	DISP
89	61		

POWER: BOILER   ENGINE
    1 Water-tube   *1 TE 5⅜ × 8 × 12/7*
                       Gas eng. in 1922

BHP (TOTAL)	SPEED (KNOTS)
256 est.	*10*

OWNERS:
N. G. Herreshoff 1902–1911
L. E. Warren 1912–1913
John K. Robinson, Jr. 1913–1915
(not listed 1916–1919)
F. A. Egan 1920–1921
F. D. M. Strachan 1922–1930

Roamer was designed by Capt. Nat Herreshoff as a comfortable cruising yacht for himself and especially for his family. As his son L. Francis Herreshoff says, she was an extremely roomy craft principally because her machinery was very compact. Her boiler was only 4'3" long by 5'0" wide. Her engine was a steeple type with the low-pressure cylinder above the other two, which with a separate camshaft alongside the crankshaft for motivating the valves, produced a short (and thus stiffer) engine. The crankcase was enclosed as it is now on nearly all reciprocating engines, whether steam, diesel, or gasoline. *Roamer* cruised comfortably on what I believe to have been less than 200 horsepower.

Roamer accommodated 18 people aft and a crew of four (captain, engineer, steward, and hand) forward. Though like most displacement vessels she rolled a bit, she was apparently comfortable in all weathers. Other than the lack of beauty, somewhat characteristic of many of Capt. Nat's designs (pipestem funnel, unattractive bow, masts too close together), *Roamer* represented an era of comfortable, silent cruising seldom found today. It is notable that later on she was reengined with a gasoline engine in 1922. As with other steam yachts of even the smallest sizes, a minimum of an engineer-cum-fireman was necessary since maneuvering controls could not be fitted at the helm as was customary in diesel or gasoline powered craft.

Roamer was not listed in Lloyd's after 1930.

TARANTULA ~ 1902

Other Names
HMCS TUNA
TUNA

DESIGNER: *Cox & King*
BUILT: *1902   By Yarrow*
MATERIAL: *Steel*   RIG: *Triple Screw Schooner*

LOA	LWL	BEAM	DRAFT in feet
153.5	152.5	15.5	7.0

GROSS TON	NET TON	TYM	DISP
123	83	172	

POWER: BOILER   ENGINE
       2 Water-tube   *3 Parsons Turbines*

BHP (TOTAL)	SPEED (KNOTS)
2500	23.30

OWNERS:
Col. Harry MacCalmont 1902–1904
W. K. Vanderbilt 1904–1914
J. K. L. Ross 1914–1916 (Tuna)
Canadian Navy World War I

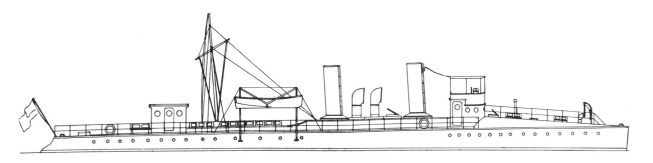

Tarantula was (except for *Turbinia* of course) one of the first high-speed turbine yachts built. Torpedo boat-like in appearance, she came to the United States and was used for commuting and trips on waters near New York for several years. She was notorious for the damages she caused by her wake when running at too high speeds on the East and Harlem Rivers. A court case was decided against Tarantula and, we believe, set the precedent that a passing vessel's owner was responsible for damages to shore front facilities and vessels moored thereto, when the passing vessel did not reduce its speed and resultant wake.

Tarantula served in the Canadian Navy as *HMCS Tuna* in World War I and did not appear in Lloyd's after that.

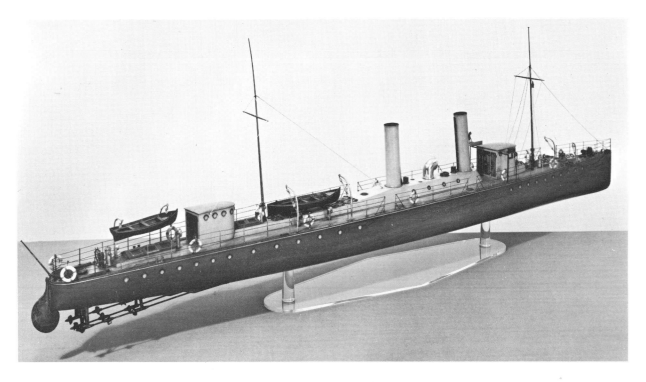

Note the nine propellers on three shafts.

TRITON ~ 1902

Other Names
RHOUMA
OSPREY
PRES. ROBERTS
HINIESTA

DESIGNER: *G. L. Watson*
BUILT: *1902* By *Ailsa SB Co.*
MATERIAL: *Steel*   RIG: *Twin Screw Schooner*

LOA	LWL	BEAM	DRAFT in feet
°*170*	*156.8*	*22.5*	*11.0*

GROSS TON	NET TON	TYM	DISP
318	*140*	*361*	

POWER BOILER   ENGINE
   1 Scotch (Oil in 1923)   *2 TE 10 × 16 × 26/18 each*
BHP (TOTAL)   SPEED (KNOTS)

   °*Lengthened 7' in 1923.*

OWNERS:
James Coats, Jr. 1902–1910
Sir George Bulloch 1911–1919 (Rhouma)
V. S. E. Grech 1920–1923
Oswald Liddell 1924–1928 (Osprey)
T. S. Manning 1929–1933
W. D. Wills 1934–1938
Sir Frederick Preston 1939–1950 (Hiniesta)
Benjamin Meaker 1951
SY Pres. Roberts Inc., Monrovia 1952–1953 (Pres. Roberts)
Camper & Nicholson 1954 (Hiniesta)
North Marine & Ind. Consult., Ltd. 1955–

Triton was one of the few steam yachts of her era with a plumb bow. Some recent advertisements state she is iron built, but a representative of her builders recently confirmed that she is steel built. In World War II she served as a calibrating vessel. Now, after over 60 years of service, she is still chartering in the Mediterranean.

HAUOLI ~ 1903

Other Names:
CALIFORNIA

DESIGNER: *H. J. Gielow*

BUILT: *1903* BY *J. N. Robins*

MATERIAL: *Steel*   RIG: *Screw Schooner*

LOA	LWL	BEAM	DRAFT in feet
211.2	166.0	22.2	8.8

GROSS TON	NET TON	TYM	DISP
299	203	412	

POWER: BOILER   ENGINE

   4 Water-tube   *1 TE 17 × 26½ × 30 × 30/21*

BHP (TOTAL)   SPEED (KNOTS)

                    18½

OWNERS:

F. M. Smith 1903–1913

Mrs. C. B. Stocker 1913–1918 (California)

US Navy World War I (Hauoli)

Hauoli was the second yacht of the same name built for F. M. Smith of 20 Mule Team Borax fame. She was a seaworthy though short-ranged yacht and of that type was reputed to be the fastest, until she challenged and raced the redoubtable *Kanahwa* for the Lysistrata Cup in 1904. *Kanahwa*, as she had done to *Noma* the year before, easily beat *Hauoli*, which then became the fastest SINGLE SCREW seagoing yacht. After some years on the east coast she was bought and taken to California. To make the trip, she was decked over and coal taken on deck as well as in her bunkers for the long voyage up the west coast of Mexico. In spite of all precautions she ran low on fuel, and had to summon the US Navy for help. The Navy was able to send a vessel and transfer sufficient coal to let *Hauoli* reach California. She went into Naval service during the war, but like many other yachts disappeared after the war. She was dropped from Lloyd's in 1920.

As mentioned above, there was another *Hauoli*, also built for Mr. Smith, also Gielow designed, and also built by Robins. This yacht was 153' LOA and was built in 1902. She later became *Seminole* and *Kajeruna*. She was also dropped from Lloyd's in 1920.

LORENA ~ 1903

Other Names
ATALANTA
KAN LU

DESIGNER: *Cox & King*
BUILT: *1903*　BY *Ramage & Ferguson*
MATERIAL: *Steel*　　RIG: *Triple Screw Schooner*

LOA	LWL	BEAM	DRAFT in feet
303	253	33.5	16.0

GROSS TON	NET TON	TYM	DISP
1303	379	1398	

POWER : BOILER　　　　　　ENGINE
　　4 Scotch　　　　*3 Parsons Turbines*
　　　　　　　　　　repowered by Diesel

BHP (TOTAL)　SPEED (KNOTS)
　3600　　　　*18*

OWNERS:
A. L. Barber 1903–1907
George J. Gould 1907–1925 (Atalanta)
War service in World War I
Chinese Government 1926–1941 (Kan Lu)

150

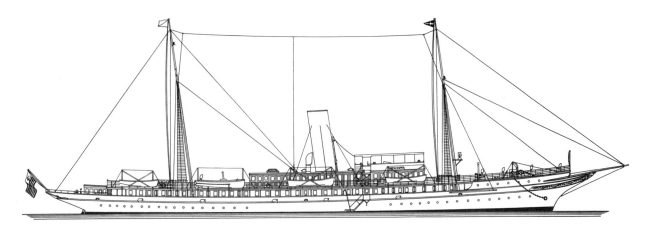

Lorena was one of the first turbine power yachts. Originally designed for two TE engines, the success of turbines in the Clyde steamer *King Edward* caused Mr. Barber to specify turbines for his yacht. She was the first Cox & King design to have her bow plating extend up to the continuation of her boat deck.

She was probably better known when she was *Atalanta*, even though her new owner George Gould used her in Europe most of the time.

In 1926 she was sold to the Chinese Government as a survey vessel. Sometime about then her turbines were removed and replaced by diesels. She remained in this service until 1941, when it is presumed that she was lost in the war with Japan. She was dropped from Jane's in 1941.

NIAGARA IV ~ 1903

Other Names
FLYER
EDNADA II

DESIGNER: *Charles L. Seabury*
BUILT: *1903*   BY *Gas Eng. & Pwr. and Seabury*
MATERIAL: *Wood*   RIG: *Twin Screw Steamer*

LOA	LWL	BEAM	DRAFT in feet
111	*104*	*12.3*	*4.3*

GROSS TON	NET TON	TYM	DISP
50	*34*		

POWER: BOILER   ENGINE
    1 Water-tube   *2 TE 8 × 12 × 20/10 each*
BHP (TOTAL)   SPEED (KNOTS)

OWNERS:
Howard Gould 1903–1909
G. C. Thomas 1909–1911 (Ednada II)
J. E. Fletcher 1911–1917 (Flyer)
W. A. Pryne 1917–1919
J. A. Nickerson 1920–1922

152

Niagara IV was one of several high-speed commuters built by Seabury. Among the others were *Little Sovereign* (2nd), *Vitesse*, and two *Vixens*, also of Seabury's designs. The photo shows *Niagara IV* in one of the rather frequent steam yacht races of that period. Racy though these yachts were, they had no cruising accommodations but were used only for commuting or day cruising in rather protected waters. In the latter 1920's a new breed of gasoline powered commuters, 50–65′LOA, with at least as good accommodations as those in the long, low steamers, were as fast as or in some cases faster (*Whim* having a speed of over 50 miles per hour), and far more maneuverable. *Niagara IV* under the name of *Flyer* lasted until 1922, when she disappeared from Lloyd's.

VENETIA ~ 1903

DESIGNER: *Cox & King*
BUILT: *1903* BY *Hawthorne & Co.*
MATERIAL: *Steel*   RIG: *Screw Schooner*

LOA	LWL	BEAM	DRAFT in feet
227	194	27.2	15.0

GROSS TON	NET TON	TYM	DISP
595	209	687	

POWER: BOILER   ENGINE
    2 Scotch (Oil in 1912)   *1 TE 16 × 26 × 42/27*
BHP (TOTAL)   SPEED (KNOTS)

OWNERS:
F. W. Sykes 1903–1904
M. F. Plant 1905–1907
Jesse Livermore 1908
G. W. Elkins 1909–1911
J. D. Spreckles 1911–1927
US Navy World War I
James Playfair 1928–1939
R. S. Misener 1940–1968

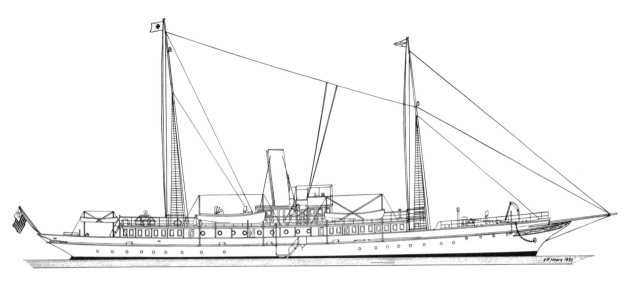

This *Venetia*, of which there were three, came to the United States and remained on this side of the Atlantic for the rest of her life. Furthermore she was always called *Venetia*. She was owned by several well-known yachtsmen but was best known under the ownership of J. D. Spreckles of sugar fame. During World War I she served out of Gibraltar, where with the help of the U.S. Coast & Geodetic Survey vessel *Surveyor*, she was credited with damaging the submarine U-39 so severely that the submarine had to seek internship in Spain. Her later years were spent in Canada on the Great Lakes. I have no record of service in World War II. She was dropped from Lloyd's in only 1968, after 65 years of service.

She was characteristic of Cox & King's designs of that era, with her funnel nearer the mainmast than the foremast, and with the top of the tall, thin funnel parallel to the waterline.

Of the two other *Venetias*, one of 1893 vintage became *North Star*, while the other, built in 1905 by Ramage & Ferguson, had several name changes but remained in the United Kingdom as a yacht.

ATLANTIC ~ 1904

DESIGNER: *William Gardner*
BUILT: *1904* BY *Townshend and Downey*
MATERIAL: *Steel* RIG: *Auxiliary 3 Masted Schooner*

LOA	LWL	BEAM	DRAFT in feet
185	139	29	18

GROSS TON	NET TON	TYM	DISP
303	203	532	

POWER: BOILER   ENGINE
    1 Water-tube   *1 TE 9 × 14 × 22½/16*

OWNERS:
Wilson Marshall 1904–1917
US Navy World War I
J. C. and N. F. Brady 1921–1923
Cornelius Vanderbilt 1924–1928
Gerard B. Lambert 1929–1942
U.S. Coast Guard World War II
W. A. and V. E. Bright 1954–1968
Al Urbelis 1969

Atlantic was probably the best known schooner yacht ever built in the United States. A really beautiful vessel, designed by Gardner, she was admired wherever seen. She was entered in the Kaiser's Cup Transatlantic Race of 1905 and from the start was the clear favorite. She was sailed by Capt. Charles Barr, easily the greatest professional skipper in the United States, though his fame had heretofore been as helmsman of such cup defenders as *Columbia*, *Reliance*, and the schooner *Ingomar* on round-the-buoy races. He drove *Atlantic* unmercifully in the Kaiser's race, to the extent that the owner and some others of the afterguard pleaded with him to reduce sail, to which he made his well-known reply, "Sir, you hired me to win this race in *Atlantic*, and that is what I will do." Fred Hoyt, a very experienced yachtsman and designer, was aboard *Atlantic* in this race and wrote a most enlightening description in Yachting of July, 1925. *Atlantic* made the 3013 miles from Sandy Hook to the Lizard in 12 days, 4 hours, 1 minute (or 11 days, 16 hours, 22 minutes to Bishops Rock), the fastest crossing ever made by a fore-and-aft rigged vessel. Her best day's run was 341 miles from noon to noon, or an average of 14.5 knots for nearly 24 hours. This compares with the clipper ship *Lightning*'s 436 miles. *Atlantic* beat *Hamburg*, the second yacht to finish, by nearly a whole day.

It is a pity that *Atlantic* never raced *Katoura*, a 162′ two-masted schooner by Herreshoff. *Katoura* was Herreshoff's largest yacht, and was built for schooner racing without power. She had *Reliance*'s mast for her mainmast, and *Constitution*'s for her foremast. Her owner, who skippered her, was not familiar with the light scientific rigging of a Herreshoff racing yacht as was a skipper like Charles Barr, so her rig was soon reduced. *Atlantic*, on the other hand, always had steam powered auxiliary and considerable comfort in her accommodation. With *Atlantic* at her fastest on a reach, and with the ability of the Herreshoff schooners to go to windward, *Katoura* would have probably beaten *Atlantic*. In the race to Spain (Ambrose Light to Santander) in 1928, *Atlantic* was beaten by 22 hours by the Herreshoff schooner *Elena*, a smaller version (136′) of *Katoura* (162′) and also fitted with auxiliary power.

Between the wars *Atlantic* was owned by Gen. Cornelius Vanderbilt and Gerard Lambert. Mr. Lambert also owned the America's Cup "J" boat *Yankee* in 1935. *Atlantic* and *Yankee* (under a reduced yawl rig) "raced" across to England that year when her owner raced *Yankee* in the "J" class while *Atlantic* acted as her mother-ship.

Atlantic served in the US Navy in World War I and was presented to the Coast Guard in World War II. She was laid up for several years after the war, until bought and turned into a "tea shop" near Wildwood, New Jersey. At least her beautiful hull and appearance could still be seen, albeit under non-yachting conditions.

In 1969, Capt. Al Urbelis bought the Atlantic and at present she is under-going repairs and refitting. She will eventually join the fleet of the Seafarer's International Union School at Piney Point, Maryland.

WARRIOR ~ 1904

Other Names
WAYFARER
GOIZEKO IZARRA

DESIGNER: *G. L. Watson*
BUILT: *1904* By *Ailsa SB Co.*
MATERIAL: *Steel*   RIG: *Twin Screw Schooner*

LOA	LWL	BEAM	DRAFT in feet
282	238.4	32.6	14.5

GROSS TON	NET TON	TYM	DISP
1098	396	1266	

POWER: BOILER   ENGINE
   2 Scotch (Oil in 1927) *2 TE 18 × 29 × 32 ×*
                                    32/27 each

BHP (TOTAL)   SPEED (KNOTS)
                            15

OWNERS:
F. W. Vanderbilt 1904–1914
A. G. Vanderbilt 1915 (Wayfarer)
Harry Payne Whitney 1916
A. S. Cochran 1916–1920 (Warrior)
British Navy World Wars I and II
Sir Ramon de la Sota 1920–1927 (Goizeko Izarra)
Rex Hayes 1938

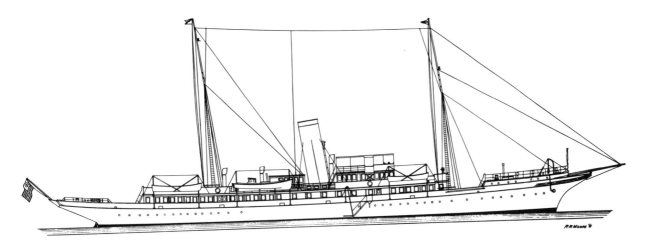

Warrior was one of Watson's largest and handsomest steam yachts. Some people claim she was Watson's best design. Of her owners, nearly all can be said to be among the most experienced on both sides of the Atlantic. In January, 1914, she was nearly lost after grounding on the Colombian coast. Her passengers had to be rescued, but after the storm subsided she was floated without much damage. She was sunk by bombing on July 11, 1940.

Another *Warrior* which might be mentioned was originally the diesel yacht *Vanadis*, 228' LOA and 1245 TYM, built by Krupp in 1924.

Goizeko Izarra is a Basque name and was used earlier for the one-time *Tuscarora* and on a former *Catarina* designed and built of iron by R. Steele in 1880, a vessel of 581 TYM.

ALBION ~ 1905

Other Names
ERIN

DESIGNER: *Sir William White*
BUILT: *1905*   By *Swan, Hunter & Wigham*
                                                           Richardson
MATERIAL: *Steel*   RIG: *Triple Screw Schooner*

LOA	LWL	BEAM	DRAFT in feet
300	*252*	*34.1*	*13.0*

GROSS TON	NET TON	TYM	DISP
1116	*403*	*1346*	

POWER: BOILER   ENGINE
              2 Scotch   *3 Parsons Turbines*
BHP (TOTAL)   SPEED (KNOTS)

OWNERS:
Sir George Newnes 1905–1908
C. L. M. Loeffler 1909–1929
Sir Thomas Lipton 1930–1935 (Erin)

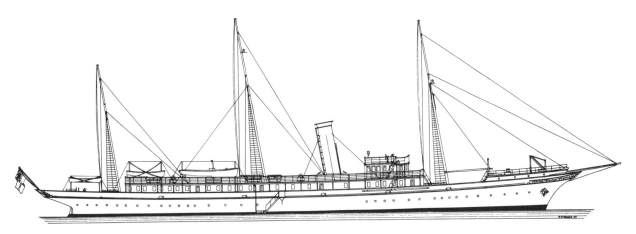

Though she was known for most of her life as *Albion*, she became more well known in the five years she was *Erin*, due to the fame (self-publicized) of her last owner, Sir Thomas Lipton. She was designed by Sir William White, who had designed the *Victoria and Albert* (3rd) in 1899, and there have always been rumors that *Albion's* design was one made for a projected Royal Yacht. In any case Sir Thomas bought her, after his previous *Erin* had been lost in World War I, to accommodate him during his last effort at the America's Cup with *Shamrock V*. She was broken up in 1936, shortly after his death. She was distinctive with her bell mouthed funnel.

CIGARETTE ~ 1905

Other Names
POCANTINO

DESIGNER: *Swasey, Raymond, and Page*
BUILT: *1905* BY *Geo. Lawley*
MATERIAL: *Steel*   RIG: *Twin Screw Steamer*

LOA	LWL	BEAM	DRAFT in feet
°126	123	14.5	4.5

GROSS TON	NET TON	TYM	DISP
99	84	120	

POWER: BOILER   ENGINE
     2 Water-tube   2 TE 8½ × 13½ × 21½ /10⅜
                            each

BHP (TOTAL)   SPEED (KNOTS)
                  22

° *Lengthened 3′ in 1911.*

OWNERS:
William H. Ames 1905–1917
US Navy World War I
Barron Collier 1921–1930 (Pocantino)

Cigarette was one of the express-type commuters, and was one of the few designed by A. Loring Swasey, who later designed so many seagoing power craft. During World War I, he was the designer of the 110′ SC sub-chasers, which were remarkable sea boats and which even now are still found in fishing fleets. During World War II, Loring Swasey again headed the small craft design section in the Navy.

Cigarette served her Boston owner for many years, but like all express steamers had little or no cruising accommodations. She was lengthened by 3′ in 1911 for reasons unknown to me, and during her life her appearance (funnels particularly) were changed. She was dropped from Lloyd's in 1930.

HONOR ~ 1905

Other Names
EROS

DESIGNER: *G. L. Watson*
BUILT: *1905* BY *Ramage & Ferguson*
MATERIAL: *Steel*   RIG: *Twin Screw Schooner*
LOA   LWL   BEAM   DRAFT in feet
260   *213*   *31.1*
GROSS TON   NET TON   TYM   DISP
915   *415*   *1020*
POWER: BOILER   ENGINE
            1 Scotch   *2 TE 13 × 21 × 34/24 each*
BHP (TOTAL)   SPEED (KNOTS)

OWNERS:
Baron de Forest 1905–1911
Baron Henri de Rothschild 1912–1915 (Eros)
French Navy World War I
Commercial interests in France 1919

Honor was the last yacht designed personally by that master of steam yacht design, George L. Watson, who died in 1904. She was unusual in that her topsides were two decks high, a covered areaway was fitted for crew's open space, and her upper deck had windows rather than portholes for the midships accommodation. In this she resembled her contemporary yacht *Queen of Scots*. She probably had more accommodation for her size than nearly any other yacht. She was chartered to Joseph Pulitzer for one cruise and he liked that experience so much that he had *Liberty* built. She was dropped from Lloyd's in 1920.

Eros is a Rothschild family name for yachts, so when *Honor* became a part of that family, her name was changed to *Eros*.

There have been at least three other *Eros* yachts. One, built in 1878, eventually became the Presidential Yacht of Liberia with the name *Lark*. Another *Eros* was a diesel yacht 213′ LOA and 915 TYM that was built for Baron Henri de Rothschild by Ramage & Ferguson in 1926. A third was the *Venetia* of 1905 (q.v.).

VENETIA ~ 1905

Other Names

EROS
TRENORA
NIKI

DESIGNER: *Cox & King*
BUILT: *1905* BY *Ramage & Ferguson*
MATERIAL: *Steel* RIG: *Screw Schooner*

LOA	LWL	BEAM	DRAFT in feet
189	166.5	26.5	14.5

GROSS TON	NET TON	TYM	DISP
577	239	568	

POWER: BOILER ENGINE
    2 Scotch *1 TE 15 × 24 × 39/27*
    (Oil in 1930)

BHP (TOTAL) SPEED (KNOTS)

OWNERS:
F. W. Sykes 1905–1913
H. Swithinbank 1913–1919, 1926–1929 (Venetia)
British Navy World Wars 1 and II
James White 1920–1921
Baron Henri de Rothschild 1922–1925 (Eros)
E. G. Stanley 1930–1932 (Trenora)
K. C. Barnaby 1933 (Venetia)
Lord Inverforth 1934–1939
Eugene Eugenides 1947 (Niki)
Fairway SS Co. 1948–1952
Home Lines, Inc. 1953–1956

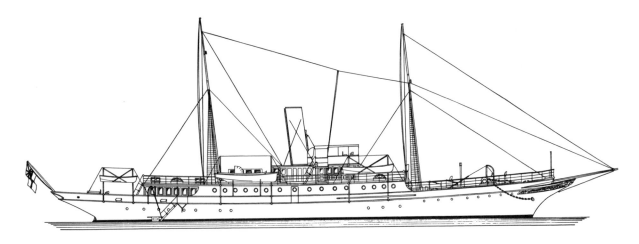

This *Venetia* is the one most often confused with Cox & King's 1903 design. They were similar in size, but this one was built by Ramage & Ferguson, while the 1903 craft was built two years before by Hawthorne. This *Venetia*, though remaining under British registry, had numerous owners and her name was changed frequently. In 1930 her amidship deck-house was extended out to the rail without a walkway on each side. In this she resembled, among others, *Tuscarora* and *Sayonara*. She appears to have been used as a charter yacht toward the end of her life. In any case, she lasted over 50 years before being dropped by Lloyd's in 1957.

AGAWA ~ 1907

Other Names
CYTHERA

DESIGNER: *Cox & King*
BUILT: *1907* BY *Ramage and Ferguson*
MATERIAL: *Steel*   RIG: *Screw Schooner*

LOA	LWL	BEAM	DRAFT in feet
215	*179.4*	*27.5*	*12.0*

GROSS TON	NET TON	TYM	DISP
602	*186*	*667*	

POWER: BOILER   ENGINE
   1 Scotch (Oil in 1938)   1 TE 17 × 27 × 31 ×
                                   31/27

BHP (TOTAL)   SPEED (KNOTS)

OWNERS:
C. W. Harkness 1907–1916
W. A. Harkness 1917–1941 (Cythera)
US Navy World Wars I and II

As *Cythera* she served in the US Navy out of Gibraltar in World War I, after which she returned to the Harkness family until she went to war again in 1942 as PY-26. While on patrol duty on the east coast of the United States she was reported missing and presumed lost. It was only after the war that the two surviving members of her crew were released from a German prison camp and reported that she had been torpedoed and sunk off the North Carolina coast in May, 1942, and that she sank so quickly that they were the only two men rescued by the submarine.

Another *Cythera* appeared during World War II in the list of patrol craft in the US Navy as PY-31. The Navy Department advises that this vessel was originally a yacht built by Krupp Germania in 1930 under the name *Abril* for Sr. Jose Ordonica y Ana attached to the Mexican Embassy in Havana. Interestingly *Abril* was never listed in either the United States or British editions of Lloyd's between 1930 and 1950, nor with the exception of *Argosy*, which later became the British *Vita*, was there any other craft built by Krupp about that time and about that size. It is possible that she was under Mexican registry and had never been listed in Lloyd's. In any case, the US Navy acquired her on July 14, 1942, and she operated in the Gulf of Mexico and on the United States east coast until placed out of service in 1946, when she was turned over to the War Shipping Administration for disposal. Eventually the Navy has determined that the second *Cythera* was actually *Argosy*. Evidently, she was sold by her British owner just before Britain entered the war, so she never appeared in Lloyd's under her new registry.

ALCYONE ~ 1907

DESIGNER: *Tams, Lemoine & Crane*
BUILT: *1907* BY *George Lawley*
MATERIAL: *Steel*   RIG: *Aux. 3-Masted Schooner*
                      Mizzen removed in 1922

OWNERS;
H. W. Putnam, Jr. 1907–1933
Commercial interests in Honduras 1934–

LOA	LWL	BEAM	DRAFT in feet
182	*140*	*30.0*	*15(with CB)*

GROSS TON	NET TON	TYM	DISP
420	*262*	*598*	

POWER: BOILER   ENGINE
         2 Water-tube   *1 TE 10 × 17 ×27/18*
                            Diesel Electric in 1922

BHP (TOTAL)   SPEED (KNOTS)

Alcyone was a comfortable cruising schooner, used extensively for this purpose. She was fortunate in being owned for her entire yachting career by the Putnams. In common with *Aloha* and some other auxiliaries, her power was changed from coal-fired steam to, in her case, diesel electric. At the same time she was rerigged and her mizzen was removed. She finally went commercial in 1934 under the Honduras flag and was dropped from Lloyd's at that time.

ALEXANDRA ~ 1907

Other Names
PRINCE OLAF

DESIGNER: *A. & J. Inglis and Admiralty*
BUILT: *1907*   BY   *A. & J. Inglis*
MATERIAL: *Steel*   RIG: *Triple Screw Schooner*

LOA	LWL	BEAM	DRAFT in feet
325	275	40.0	13.0

GROSS TON	NET TON	TYM	DISP
1728		2157	2050

POWER: BOILER   ENGINE
         3 Water-tube   *3 Parsons Turbines*

BHP (TOTAL)	SPEED (KNOTS)
4500	18.8

OWNERS:
British Navy as Royal Yacht 1907–1922
Commercial interests 1925

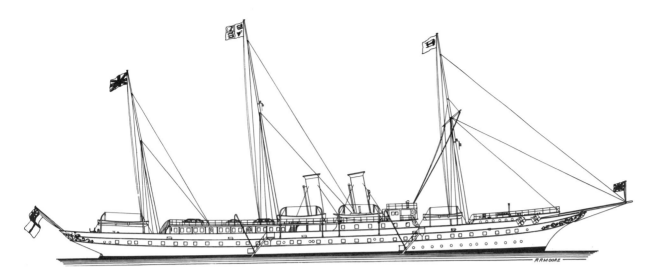

Alexandra was built for and used by King Edward VII and later by King George V. She replaced the *Osborne* (3rd). Though resembling the then current *Victoria and Albert* (3rd) she was only one-third the latter's tonnage. She made many cross-channel trips and at least one to Sweden.

King George V's great love was racing in sail and every moment he could spare he would try to be aboard his beloved *Britannia*. So he had little use for two large steam yachts. It was finally decided to retain the older but larger and more famous *Victoria and Albert* as the Royal Yacht and to dispose of the *Alexandra*. She was sold in 1925 and became a Norwegian cruise boat. She was destroyed during the invasion of Norway in 1940.

WAKIVA ~ 1907

DESIGNER: *Cox & King*
BUILT: *1907* BY *Ramage & Ferguson*
MATERIAL: *Steel*   RIG: *Twin Screw Schooner*

LOA	LWL	BEAM	DRAFT in feet
239	195.5	30.8	13.9

GROSS TON	NET TON	TYM	Disp
853	337	909	

POWER: BOILER   ENGINE
      2 Scotch   *2 TE 15 × 24 × 39/27 each*
BHP (TOTAL)   SPEED (KNOTS)

OWNERS:
L. V. and H. S. Harkness 1907–1917
US Navy World War I

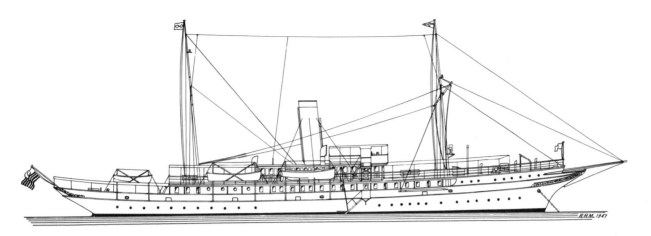

Wakiva was another typical Cox & King yacht of the early 1900's. These were almost standardized in design, and especially in appearance. She was fortunate in having only one owner during her yachting career. She was turned over to the Navy in World War I, and formed part of the Breton Patrol. Unfortunately she was sunk in collision off Brest on May 22, 1918, while on convoy duty.

She was another yacht that had the plating of the bow extended to a continuation of the boat deck forward.

There was a previous Wakiva, also owned by L. V. Harkness, also designed by Cox & King, also built by Ramage & Ferguson. She was built in 1903, was 192' LOA and 488 TYM (417GT). Mr. Harkness did not sell her until 1913. She was dropped from Lloyd's in 1915.

WINCHESTER ~ 1907

DESIGNER: *H. J. Gielow*

BUILT: *1907* BY *Robert Jacob*

MATERIAL: *Steel* RIG: *Twin Screw Steamer*

LOA	LWL	BEAM	DRAFT in feet
141.5	140	15.5	5.5

GROSS TON	NET TON	TYM	DISP
147	100	158	

POWER: BOILER ENGINE

     2 Water-tube *2 TE 12 × 18 × 20 × 20/15*
                            each

BHP (TOTAL) SPEED (KNOTS)
                        21

OWNERS:

P. W. Rouss 1907–1909

A. G. Vanderbilt 1909–1916 (Adroit)

I. E. Emerson 1916–1928

Barron Collier 1929–1937, 1939–1941 (Aera)

Melville Cannon 1938

This *Winchester* was the first of four large, fast, steam yachts, each bigger than pure commuters, yet with limited accommodations. As these four were all built between 1907 and 1915, they became one of the best known families of yachts in the United States. Her owner was the son of a Charles Broadway Rouss, of Winchester, Virginia, who from dealing in scrap and job-lot materials, built a huge business. He became a philanthropist, giving lavishly to Con-federate Army memorials (in which he had served) and to his birthplace, Winchester, Virginia.

After being "bitten" by the fast-steamer bug Peter Winchester Rouss soon ordered another yacht. This second *Winchester* and the others resembled, to a growing degree, naval destroyers. Her succeeding owners kept her for considerable periods of time. She was finally dropped from Lloyd's after 1941.

CASSANDRA ~ 1908

Other Names
CASIANA
BANAHAW

DESIGNER: *A. S. Chesborough*
BUILT: *1908* By *Scott SB & Eng., Ltd.*
MATERIAL: *Steel* RIG: *Twin Screw Schooner*

LOA	LWL	BEAM	DRAFT in feet
287	239	33.0	15.5

GROSS TON	NET TON	TYM	DISP
1227	551	1280	

POWER: BOILER   ENGINE
    2 Water-tube   *2 TE 16 × 26 ×*
    (Oil in 1915)   *42/27 each*
BHP (TOTAL)   SPEED (KNOTS)

OWNERS:
Roy Rainey 1908–1912
G. J. Whelan 1913–1915
E. L. Doheny 1916–1936 (Casiana)
US Navy World War I
Philippine Govt. 1937–1941 (Banahaw)

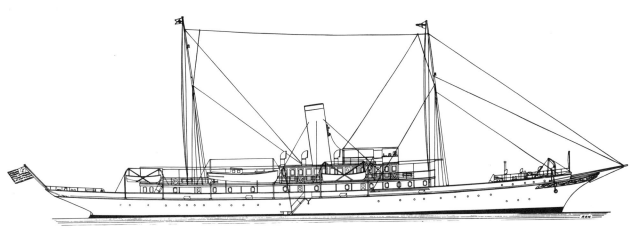

Cassandra was one of several yachts designed by Chesborough, one of the popular designers of his day. Though she was built in Britain, most of his designs were built in the United States. Her original owners used her for extensive cruises to Africa and South America, where they engaged in big game hunting and mountain climbing. Figure 1 shows her crew.

Purchased by Mr. Doheny, she went to the West Coast, where she made many voyages to Hawaii and to Alaskan waters. She was sold to the Philippine Government as a yacht in 1937. She was apparently renamed *Banahaw*, but the name didn't catch on and she was evidently known as *Casania*. It has been reported that she was bombed and sunk by the Japanese off Corregidor Island in 1942.

IOLANDA ~ 1908

Other Names
HMS WHITE BEAR

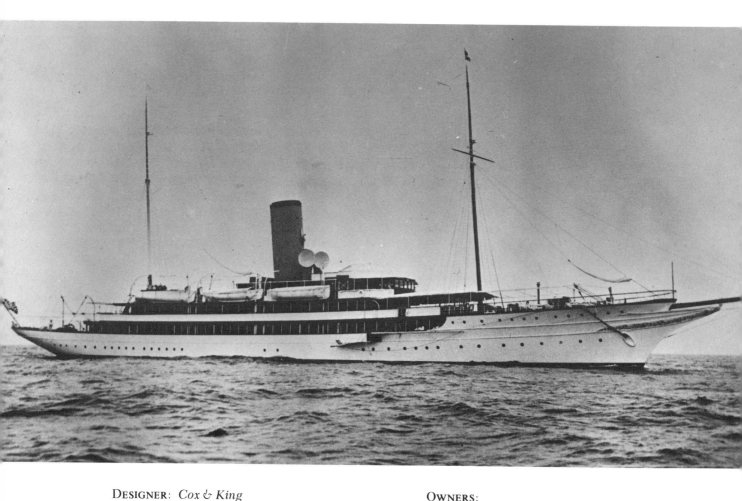

DESIGNER: *Cox & King*
BUILT: *1908* By *Ramage & Ferguson*
MATERIAL *Steel* RIG: *Twin Screw Schooner*

LOA	LWL	BEAM	DRAFT in feet
318	*275.2*	*37.5*	*16.0*

GROSS TON	NET TON	TYM	DISP
1647	*723*	*1848*	

POWER: BOILER ENGINE
2 Water-tube, 2 Scotch *2TE 19 × 31 × 35 ×*
(Oil in 1927) *35/27 each*

BHP (TOTAL)	SPEED (KNOTS)
4000	*19*

OWNERS:
M. F. Plant 1909–1911
Mme. E. Terestchenko 1912–1919
British Navy World Wars I and II
Camper & Nicholson 1920–1927
Mr. and Mrs. Moses Taylor 1928–1939
Commercial interests 1947

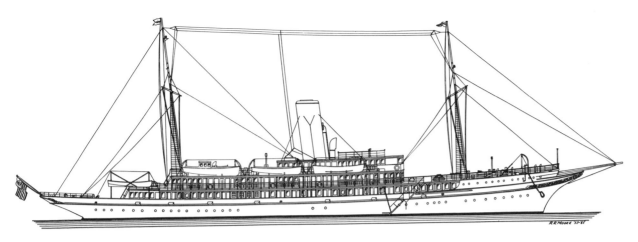

Iolanda was one of the most distinctive yachts of her time. She was rather different in appearance from most of Cox & King's designs. Her high superstructure, her large and tall yet graceful funnel, all made her outstanding in any group of large yachts. Shortly after her commissioning, her owner, already experienced with several yachts, took her on an extended voyage of 33,000 miles to the Mediterranean and eastward as far as Japan before returning again to the Mediterranean and to the United States. Whether it is a fact or simply coincidence, Morton Plant owned at the same time the fast Herreshoff schooner *Elena*, the name of the then Queen of Italy, and the steam yacht *Iolanda*, the name of the Italian Princess Royal.

Morton Plant, a prominent owner of East Coast and Caribbean shipping lines, had sold his interests and devoted himself to yachting for some years. He had owned the fast Herreshoff schooner *Ingomar* while she campaigned in Europe in 1904 under Charles Barr, and later had *Elena* built to compete with A. S. Cochran's *Westward*. Meanwhile his seagoing comforts were appeased by such steam yachts as *Venetia* (1903), *Iolanda*, and later *Kanahwa*, *Vanadis*, etc.

After World War I she was managed by Camper & Nicholson as a charter yacht pending a sale to a new owner, who became Mr. Moses Taylor of New York's National City Bank. After his death, Mrs. Taylor kept this comfortable yacht until World War II when she operated in the British Navy as a survey ship. After the war she was sold into commercial service in 1947. So ended the yachting life of one of the most distinctive and grandest yachts of her era.

LIBERTY ~ 1908

Other Names
GLENCAIRN

DESIGNER: *G. L. Watson & Co.*
BUILT: *1908* BY *Ramage & Ferguson*
MATERIAL: *Steel* RIG: *Twin Screw Schooner*

LOA	LWL	BEAM	DRAFT in feet
304	*250*	*36.5*	*16.0*

GROSS TON	NET TON	TYM	DISP
1607	*895*	*1791*	

POWER: BOILER ENGINE
1 Scotch *2 TE 16 × 26 × 42/24 each*

BHP (TOTAL) SPEED (KNOTS)
15¾

OWNERS:
Joseph Pulitzer 1908–1912
James Ross 1912–1913 (Glencairn)
Lord Tredeger 1914–1915 (Liberty)
British Navy World War I (as hospital ship)
Sir Robert and Lady Houston 1920–1937

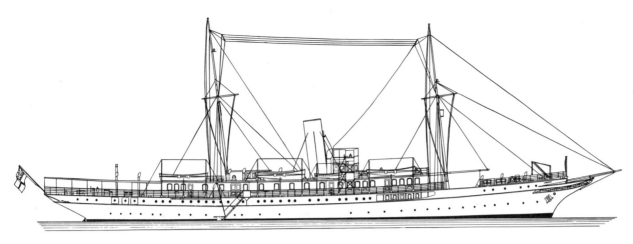

Liberty was designed by Watson's firm and built with many distinctive characteristics for Joseph Pulitzer, the very successful newspaper publisher of not only his St. Louis papers, but the New York World, which he had built into one of the then great newspapers of the United States. Mr. Pulitzer suffered from near blindness, though unkind critics often said he could see quite well when necessary. In any case his purblindness, enhanced by an acute hearing and a high-strung temperment, made him most susceptible to any unfamiliar noise. He had chartered yachts and found relative peace and quiet aboard. *Liberty* was designed to insulate her owner from every possible extraneous noise. Considering the limitations on the art of soundproofing over 60 years ago, everything was done to isolate her owner's quarters from any sound. The yacht was also designed to avoid any sharp corners in passages where handrails, were fitted, and no steps, breaks in deck, doorjambs, or other obstructions to easy movement were permitted. They tell of a secretary who was assigned to the owner's cabin, while fitting out, to test its soundproofing. He was kept awake by a hammering sound, which in the morning turned out to be the jack and rivet hammers at work, on a 24 hour basis, on an ocean liner undergoing urgent repairs in an adjacent berth. She evidently gave her owner the nocturnal peace he sought. She eventually served as a hospital ship in World War I, and after the war was owned by the Houstons. Lady Houston, her last owner, was probably best remembered as the donor of sufficient funds to permit Britain, in aircraft flown by the Royal Air Force, to enter and win forever the Schneider Trophy for seaplane racing.

Liberty was eventually broken up about 1937.

VANADIS ~ 1908

DESIGNER: *Tams, Lemoine & Crane*
BUILT: *1908* BY *A. & J. Inglis*
MATERIAL: *Steel* RIG: *Triple Screw Schooner*

LOA	LWL	BEAM	DRAFT in feet
277.5	232	32.6	14.0

GROSS TON	NET TON	TYM	DISP
1092	516	1233	

POWER: BOILER   ENGINE
      2 Scotch   *3 Turbines. Center one*
   (Oil in 1927) *replaced by TE Engine in 1910*

BHP (TOTAL)	SPEED (KNOTS)
3000	16.4

OWNERS:
C. K. G. Billings 1908–1915
M. F. Plant 1916
Russian Navy 1917–1919 (Poryvz)
Baron de Linder (Finlandia) 1919–1921
Mme. Virginie Heriot 1922–1924
M. Grahame-White 1925–1935 (Ianara)
Commercial Service 1936–1938

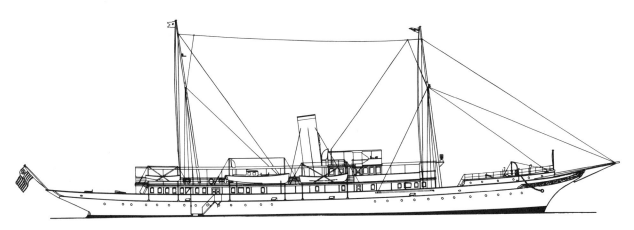

Vanadis was the largest yacht designed by that most competent and artistic engineer Clinton Crane. Her owner wished her to be powered with the comparatively new (then) turbine drive. Clinton Crane describes her limitations in fuel capacity for westbound transatlantic trips. The most economical speed was computed and off she started for the United States. After several days the chief engineer found that scaffolding had not been removed from a major bunker so the bunker was nowhere near as full as expected. Because turbines become more and more inefficient at lower speeds, a critical situation occurred, since to go to the Azores or even Halifax would have been a black mark against this new and large yacht's power by the new turbines. Eventually she was able to reach New London under her own power.

Vanadis was one of the most comfortable yachts afloat. Some years after World War I, in which she served in the British and Russian Navies, she was bought by Montague Grahame-White, brother of Claude Grahame-White, the famous prewar aviator. M. Grahame-White had, for some years, quite a fleet of large yachts for charter. While under charter, they provided a good profit, but periods of layup ate into the profits to the extent that, until he was able to sell such yachts for commercial or war use, he was forced to sell his estate on the Hamble River. After commercial service, Vanadis was reported to have been broken up in 1938.

Another Vanadis, designed by Cox & Stevens and built by Krupp in 1924, of 1245 TYM, was later called Warrior. She was diesel powered.

VISITOR II ~ 1908

Other Names
GUINEVERE

DESIGNER: *Swasey, Raymond & Page*
BUILT: *1908* By *George Lawley*
MATERIAL: *Steel* RIG: *Aux. 3 Masted Schooner*

LOA	LWL	BEAM	DRAFT in feet
197.5	150	32.5	17.0

GROSS TON	NET TON	TYM	DISP
499	296	779	

POWER: BOILER   ENGINE
   1 Scotch *1 TE 14½ × 24 × 38/22*
BHP (TOTAL) SPEED (KNOTS)

OWNERS:
W. H. Brown 1908–1911
Edgar Palmer 1912, 1914–1917 (Guinevere)
R. P. Doremus 1913
US Navy World War I

This yacht was best known as *Guinevere*. The orange and black private signal of Mr. Palmer demonstrated his loyalty to Princeton University, to whom he gave its Palmer Football Stadium. Unfortunately she was wrecked in naval service during the war.

After the war, Edgar Palmer had another three-masted schooner designed by Swasey and built by Lawley. This second *Guinevere* was one of the first yachts built with a diesel-electric power plant.

LITTLE SOVEREIGN (2nd) ~ 1909

Other Names
SOVEREIGN
VEREIGN

DESIGNER: *Charles L. Seabury*
BUILT: *1909* By *Gas Eng. & Pow. and Seabury*
MATERIAL: : *Wood*   RIG: *Twin Screw Steamer*

LOA	LWL	BEAM	DRAFT in feet
137	*127*	*13.5*	*4.5*

GROSS TON	NET TON	TYM	DISP
91	*61*	*110*	

POWER: BOILER   ENGINE
        *1 Water-tube   2 TE 10½ × 16½ × 18½ ×
                        18½/11 each*

BHP (TOTAL)	SPEED (KNOTS)
	24

OWNERS:
M. C. D. Borden 1909–1911
C. L. Seabury 1911–1917
F. W. White 1917–1922
(Not listed 1923) (Sovereign)
John Hart 1924 (Vereign)

This *Little Sovereign*, designed and built by Seabury, succeeded the first *Little Sovereign*, a Herreshoff steamer of 1904. The Herreshoff craft had one funnel and a pointed canoe stern. When replaced by this vessel she became the *Sioux*. This craft had three funnels close together and a counter stern. She was easily confused with *Vitesse*, built the following year. Her owner used her for commuting from his home in New Jersey to New York City and to visit the Borden cotton mills in Fall River, Massachusetts, 150-odd miles from New York. She remained in his service for less than two years until, when overhauled and passed by the second *Winchester*, her owner, in the grand manner, merely told his captain not to let him off at the New York Yacht Club landing on the East River, but to continue to Morris Heights on the Harlem River to place an order with Seabury for a faster yacht.

After World War I she drifted into and became one of the better known rumrunners before being captured by the Coast Guard. She was dropped from Lloyd's in 1924.

TRIAD ~ 1909

DESIGNER: *Caledonian SB, Ltd.*
BUILT: *1909* BY *Caledonian SB, Ltd.*
MATERIAL: *Steel*   RIG: *Twin Screw Schooner*

LOA	LWL	BEAM	DRAFT in feet
250	240	35.2	

GROSS TON	NET TON	TYM	DISP
1182	427	1412	

POWER: BOILER   ENGINE
        2 Scotch   *2 TE 20 × 33¼ × 52½/36 each*

BHP (TOTAL)   SPEED (KNOTS)
    2235

OWNERS:
G. A. Schenley 1909–1912
R. A. Grech 1913
British Navy 1914–

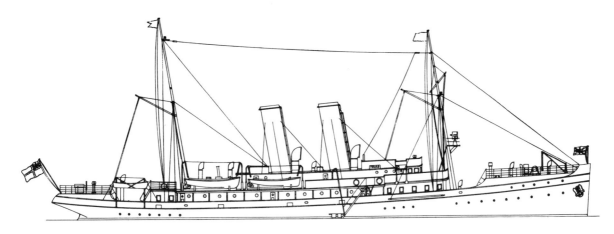

At the outbreak of World War I, *Triad* was cruising in the eastern Mediterranean. She was taken over by the British Navy and was present at Gallipoli. When on May 25, 1915, a German submarine approached the Allied fleet, Admiral de Roebeck ordered the battleships to clear those waters and he transferred his flag to *Triad*. She was his flagship during the Gallipoli Campaign. Thereafter she remained as the flagship in those waters. Later she operated in the Persian Gulf waters.

WINCHESTER (2nd) ~ 1909

Other Names
FLYING FOX
MARISCAL SUCRE

DESIGNER: *Cox & King*
BUILT: *1909* BY *Yarrow*
MATERIAL: *Steel*   RIG: *Triple Screw Steamer*

LOA	LWL	BEAM	DRAFT in feet
165.5	165	15.5	5.5

GROSS TON	NET TON	TYM	DISP
		188	125

POWER: BOILER   ENGINE
    2 Water-tube (Oil)   3 Parsons Turbines

BHP (TOTAL)	SPEED (KNOTS)
2500	25

OWNERS:
P. W. Rouss 1909–1912
Irving Cox, et al. 1913–1915 (Flying Fox)
C. K. G. Billings 1916–1920
Dr. J. A. Harriss 1920–1929
W. B. Leeds 1930–1937
Colombian Navy 1938–1955 (Mariscal Sucre)

This *Winchester* was the second of a family of four fast yachts. She was more destroyer-like in her appearance and was a distinct improvement over the first *Winchester*. Not satisfied, her owner soon ordered a third vessel. This one was later owned by three experienced and well-known yachtsmen. Eventually she was sold to the Colombian Navy where she served 17 years. She was dropped from Jane's in 1955 after over 40 years of life.

ALOHA (2nd) ~ 1910

DESIGNER: *Tams, Lemoine & Crane*
BUILT: *1910* By *Fore River SB & Eng. Co.*
MATERIAL: *Steel* RIG: *Auxiliary Bark*

LOA	LWL	BEAM	DRAFT in feet
216	*165.8*	*35.6*	*17.5*

GROSS TON	NET TON	TYM	DISP
659	*369*	*878*	

POWER: BOILER   ENGINE
       2 Water-tube   *1 TE 12 × 19 × 30/24*
                  Diesel-electric in 1927

BHP (TOTAL)   SPEED (KNOTS)

OWNERS:
Arthur Curtiss James 1910–1938
US Navy World War I

194

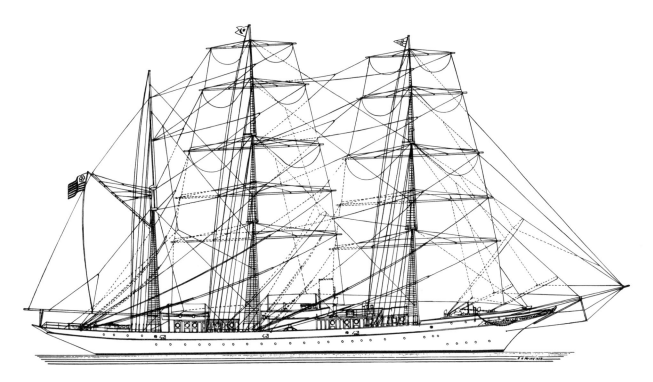

Aloha was built to replace Aloha (1st), a brigantine also designed by Clinton Crane, in which her owner had cruised extensively. Arthur Curtiss James was one of the comparatively few American yacht owners to make extensive cruises at that time. (Aloha the brigantine made at least 12 transatlantic crossings.) In this he resembled Lord Brassey. Aloha (2nd), the bark, became one of the best known and loved yachts in the United States. Mr. James owned her for her entire life except for her naval service in World War I. She made at least 16 transatlantic crossings, visiting the Baltic and Mediterranean Seas as well as making a round-the world voyage in 1921–1922. A yacht like Aloha carried a rather large crew as she was often on long cruises. For her trip around the world she had her captain, two mates, a boatswain, a carpenter, a radio man, and 16 hands. Her engine room staff comprised a chief engineer, two assistants, two oilers, and two firemen. There

were nine in the stewards department including a stewardess. A doctor was part of the afterguard on all extensive voyages. Aloha's design, based on experience with Aloha (1st), was laid out particularly for ocean voyages. Her forward deckhouse had the chartroom, galley, and stairway, while the after one had a commodious saloon and stairway to the cabins. There were six large staterooms as well as rooms for the doctor and the maid. She had a separate sickbay, where a patient could be isolated, as well as a laundry.

She was scrapped in 1938 after 28 years of loyal service.

Unfortunately there was a typographical error in "Clinton Crane's Yachting Memories," written by her designer, in which he says she was built by "Fall River Engine Co." She was actually built at Fore River, the well-known yard in Quincy, Massachusetts.

DORIS ~ 1910

Other Names
EILEEN
GIRUNDIA II

DESIGNER: *G. L. Watson & Co.*
BUILT: *1910*   BY   *John Brown, Ltd.*
MATERIAL: *Steel*   RIG: *Twin Screw Schooner*
LOA   LWL   BEAM   DRAFT: *in feet*
270   *222*   *30.9*   *15.5*
GROSS TON   NET TON   TYM   DISP
910   *383*   *1022*
POWER: BOILER   ENGINE
   1 Scotch (Oil in 1921)   2 TE 16 × 26 × 30 ×
                                      30/26 each
BHP (TOTAL)   SPEED (KNOTS)

OWNERS:
Solomon B. Joel 1910–1931 (name changed to Eileen
   in 1914)
Pierre duPuy 1932–1948 (Girundia II)
French Navy World War II

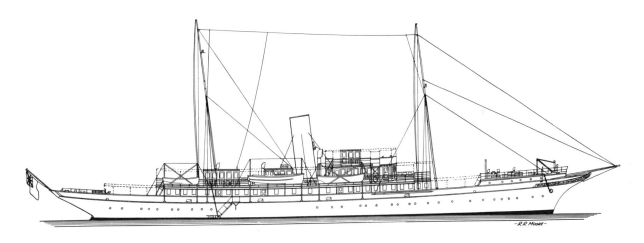

This *Doris* replaced another *Doris*, built by Ramage & Ferguson in 1896 of 530 gross tons that later became *Iolaire*, not the Beardmore built one.

This *Doris* was a sister to *Jeannette*, built the fol-lowing year.

She served as the flagship of the French admiral at L'Orient during part of World War II. She was dropped from Lloyd's in 1949.

MIRANDA ~ 1910

Other Names
MIRANDA II
PATRICIA

DESIGNER: *C. E. Nicholson*
BUILT: *1910* By *Camper & Nicholson (Hull by Thornycroft)*
MATERIAL: *Steel*   RIG: *Twin Screw Schooner*

LOA	LWL	BEAM	DRAFT in feet
230	*190.3*	*31.8*	

GROSS TON	NET TON	TYM	DISP
793	*364*	*940*	

POWER: BOILER   ENGINE
         2 Scotch   *2 TE 14½ × 23½ ×38/24 each*
BHP (TOTAL)   SPEED (KNOTS)

OWNERS:
Lord Leith 1910–1915
British Navy World Wars I and II
Trinity House 1919–1939 (Patricia)

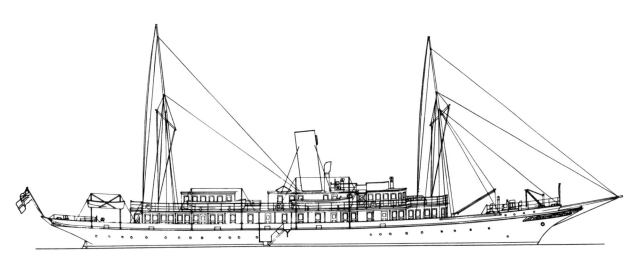

Miranda, similar to Nicholson's *Marynthea* of the following year, was probably best known as *Patricia* under which name she served for many years as the Trinity House Yacht and played a prominent part in several Fleet Reviews when she led the reviewing vessel through the Fleet.

VITESSE ~ 1910

Other Names
SKIPAKI
GREYHOUND

DESIGNER: *Charles L. Seabury*
BUILT: *1919* By *Gas Eng. & Pwr., Seabury*
MATERIAL: *Composite*   RIG: *Twin Screw Steamer*

LOA	LWL	BEAM	DRAFT in feet
140	133	13.8	4.5

GROSS TON	NET TON	TYM	DISP
103	70		

POWER: BOILER   ENGINE
     1 Water-tube   *2 TE 11 × 16 × 18 × 18/11*
                              each

BHP (TOTAL)   SPEED (KNOTS)

OWNERS:
Brayton Ives 1910–1915
Henry P. Davison 1916–1919 (Skipaki)
Dr. J. A. Harriss 1920–1926 (Greyhound)

Vitesse was a spendid example of a fast commuter of her era. She resembled, with her three closely spaced funnels, the second *Little Sovereign* (137′ LOA). Other similar yachts also designed by Seabury were *Niagara IV* (111′ LOA–1903), the first *Vixen* (118′ LOA–1903), and the somewhat longer second *Vixen* (167′ LOA–1913). *Vitesse* spent most of her life as a commuter and day sailer around Long Island Sound. She was dropped from Lloyd's after 1929.

JEANNETTE ~ 1911

Other Names
SAINT MODWEN

DESIGNER: *G. L. Watson & Co*

BUILT: *1911   By John Brown, Ltd.*

MATERIAL: *Steel*   RIG: *Twin Screw Schooner*

LOA	LWL	BEAM	DRAFT in feet
270	222	31.3	15.5

GROSS TON	NET TON	TYM	DISP
931	396	1023	

POWER: BOILER   ENGINE

　　　　1 Scotch   2 TE 16 × 26 × 30 × 30/26 each

BHP (TOTAL)   SPEED (KNOTS)

OWNERS:

Sir Harry Livesay 1911–1936

Wm. Lancaster 1937

John Gretton 1938–1939

　　Naval service in World Wars I and II unknown

　　Commercial 1946 "Saint Modwen"

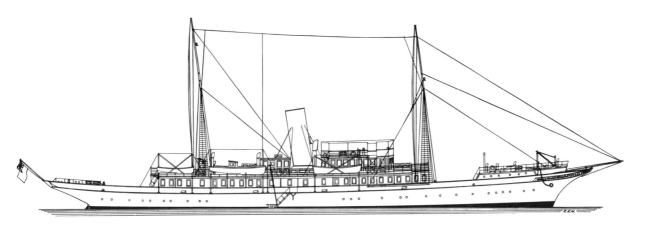

Jeannette was practically a sister of *Doris* 1910. I understand that her original owner tried to have the builder copy *Doris* without reference to the de-signer. When the builder refused, he went to G. L. Watson & Co., and minor changes were incorporated.

MARYNTHEA ~ 1911

DESIGNER: *C. E. Nicholson*
BUILT: *1911 By Camper & Nicholson*
                    (Hull Thornycroft)

MATERIAL: *Steel*   RIG: *Twin Screw Schooner*

LOA	LWL	BEAM	DRAFT in feet
233	193.5	30.6	13.5

GROSS TON	NET TON	TYM	DISP
853	338	900	

POWER: BOILER   ENGINE
2 Water-tube (Oil in 1937)   2 TE 15 × 23½ ×
                                    38/24 each

BHP (TOTAL)   SPEED (KNOTS)
   1860 est.

OWNERS:
H. J. Mason 1911–1915
British Navy World Wars I and II
Lord Furness 1919 (Emerald)
Sir Arthur and P. H. du Cros 1920–1926
H. Gordon Selfridge 1927–1934 (Conqueror)
Sir Hugo Cunliff-Owen 1935–1947
Commercial interests 1948

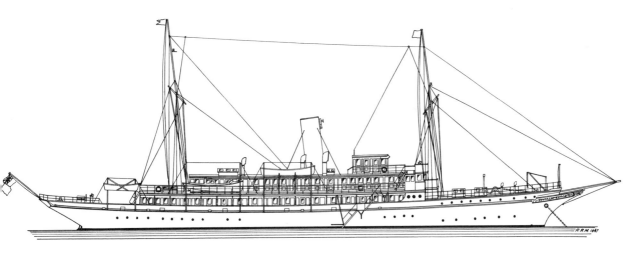

Marynthea was one of Nicholson's early steam yacht designs. The hulls for these early steam yachts were subcontracted to Thornycroft. Though Nicholson was probably better known for his sailing yachts between the wars, he did design, and his yard built many successful diesel yachts including *Philante*. *Marynthea's* original owner was an ardent fisherman, so the yacht spent considerable time in Scandinavian waters. After World War I she became well known around the coast of Great Britain. During World War II she served as an anti-aircraft vessel and was known as HMS *Conqueror II*, because one of the projected battleships that was never built was to have been HMS *Conqueror*, an historical name in the Royal Navy. She went into commercial service in 1948.

Another yacht *Conqueror* had been built in 1889. Though also well known, the difference in their ages and the fact that the older one spent most of her life in the United States, prevents confusion between the two.

SOVEREIGN ~ 1911

DESIGNER: *Charles L. Seabury*
BUILT: *1911   By Gas Eng. & Pwr. Co. and*
C. L. Seabury
MATERIAL: *Bronze and Steel*   RIG: *Triple Screw*
Steamer

LOA	LWL	BEAM	DRAFT in feet
166	160.5	16.5	4.5

GROSS TON	NET TON	TYM	DISP
173	118		

POWER: BOILER   ENGINE
    2 Water-tube   *2 TE 13½ × 20¾ × 26½ ×*
    (Oil in 1913)   *26½ / 13½ each;*
        3 Curtis-turbines in 1913;
        1 Turb. removed 1914

BHP (TOTAL)   SPEED (KNOTS)
6000 (3 turb.)   *38 (3 Turb.)*

OWNERS:
M. C. D. and B. & H. Borden 1911–1920

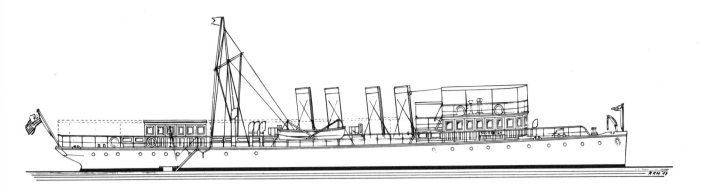

This extreme craft was usually referred to as the "fast *Sovereign*" to distinguish her from her predecessors the two *Little Sovereigns*, and further back, the big cruising steam yacht *Sovereign*. As referred to under *Little Sovereign* (1909), her owner, annoyed at being overhauled and passed by one of the *Winchesters*, simply told the captain of *Little Sovereign* not to drop him off at the New York Yacht Club landing on the East River, but to continue on to Seabury's yard so he could order a faster yacht. This *Sovereign* was the result.

After a short period of use her twin reciprocating engines were replaced by three Curtis turbines. In this form she was said to have made 38 knots, or faster than *Turbinia* and the third (and fastest) *Winchester*, but less than *Arrow's* speed on her famous trial. She was also unique in having four funnels—I believe the only yacht so fitted.

I understand that she could only hold her high speed for a short period of time, due to boiler limitations. So after a year her center turbine was removed.

There is very little data published on this, one of the most interesting of yachts. Even photographs are hard to find. One would think that such a unique and distinctive craft would have been described in technical journals. If any readers have anything to contribute on the vessel I would appreciate whatever can be sent to me.

SAPPHIRE ~ 1912

Other Names
HMS BREDA

DESIGNER: *G. L. Watson & Co.*
BUILT: *1912* By *John Brown*
MATERIAL: *Steel*   RIG: *Twin Screw Schooner*

LOA	LWL	BEAM	DRAFT in feet
285	242	35.2	14.0

GROSS TON	NET TON	TYM	DISP
1207	546	1421	

POWER: BOILER   ENGINE
 2 Scotch (Oil in 1920)   *2 TE 18 × 29 ×*
                   32 × 32/27 each

BHP (TOTAL)   SPEED (KNOTS)
                   14.0

OWNERS:
Duke of Bedford 1912–1919
British Navy World Wars I and II (HMS Breda)
Lord Furness 1920–1923
Urban Broughton (later Lord Fairhaven) 1924–1939

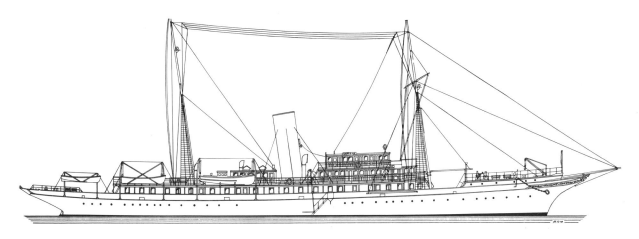

Sapphire was one of the handsomest, most comfortable, and seaworthy yachts ever designed by Watson's firm. A study of her plan and profile (Fig. 5) will show the state of the art in 1912. Though she had two experienced owners before Mr. Broughton, and was used rather extensively by the Duchess of Bedford before World War I, it was under Mr. Broughton's ownership that *Sapphire* was probably best known. He was a brilliant civil engineer in the United Kingdom, Canada, and the United States.

He married the daughter of H. H. Rogers, owner of the Virginian Railroad in the United States, and of the fast steam yacht *Kanahwa*. The Broughtons cruised extensively in *Sapphire*, to the Orient and back one year, to the West Indies another, etc.

Sapphire served out of Gibraltar during World War I, and as HMS *Breda* a submarine tender in World War II. She was sunk in a collision on February 18, 1944.

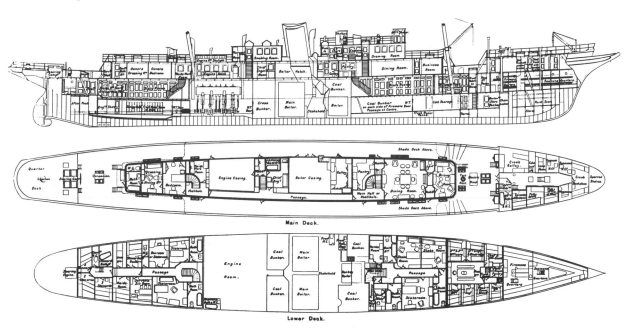

WINCHESTER (3rd) ~ 1912

Other Names
TRILLORA
GRILSE

DESIGNER: *Cox & Stevens*
BUILT: *1912*   BY *Yarrow*
MATERIAL: *Steel*   RIG: *Twin Screw Steamer*

LOA	LWL	BEAM	DRAFT in feet
205	204	18.5	6.0

GROSS TON	NET TON	TYM	DISP
291	198	340	

POWER: BOILER   ENGINE
    2 Water-tube, Oil   2 Yarrow Turbines

BHP (TOTAL)	SPEED (KNOTS)
7000	32

OWNERS:
P. W. Rouss 1912–1915
S. R. Guggenheim 1922–1938 (Trillora)
Merritt, Chapman & Scott 1939–1941
Canadian Navy World War I HMCS GRILSE

This was the third of four famous *Winchesters*. She was considerably larger than her predecessor, though most of the increase in space was devoted to the big increase in power. She provided her owner with a dining room and small lounge on deck, while below were the owner's cabin and bath, a tiny hall off which opened one small double and two tiny single cabins all sharing one bath.

This *Winchester* really looked like a destroyer, as did her successor, which incidentally was hard to distinguish from this *Winchester*, both having been designed by Cox & Stevens.

Like many other yachts she did not reappear in Lloyd's after World War II.

CYPRUS ~ 1913

DESIGNER: *Cox & Stevens*
BUILT: *1913* BY *Seattle Const. Co. (Skinner &*
Eddy)
MATERIAL: *Steel*   RIG: *Twin Screw Schooner*

LOA	LWL	BEAM	DRAFT in feet
°266.8	250	28.0	12.5

GROSS TON	NET TON	TYM	DISP
1286	874		

POWER: BOILER   ENGINE
Water-tube, Oil 2 *TE 16 × 24 × 30 × 30/24 each*

BHP (TOTAL)	SPEED (KNOTS)
	19

OWNERS:
D. C. Jackling 1913–1917
Russian Navy 1917

Lengthened 34'10'' in 1914. Second funnel added.

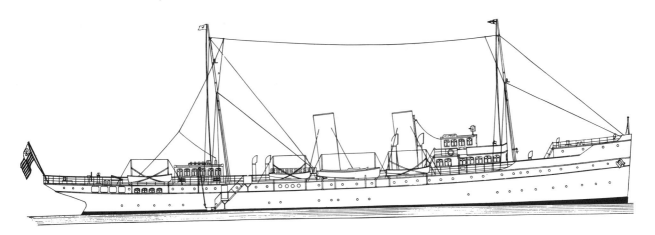

Cyprus was unusual as, contrary to most large yachts at that time, she was built on the West Coast, instead of near New York or in Britain. Her owner had large copper interests. When she first went into service, she appeared to "squat" aft. Whether for this reason or others, she was soon lengthened, and a second funnel added, as had been done in *Noma*. Altered, she became a good-looking and fairly satisfactory yacht, until 1917 when she was bought for and entered the Russian Navy. There has been no information on her since then.

ERSATZ HOHENZOLLERN ~ 1913

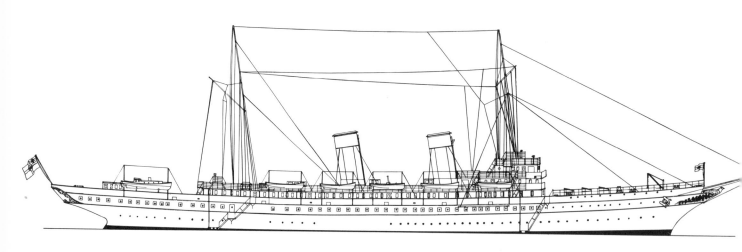

DESIGNER: *German Admiralty*

BUILT: *1913* BY *Vulcan*

MATERIAL: *Steel*   RIG: *Triple Screw Schooner*

LOA	LWL	BEAM	DRAFT in feet
520 est.	*437 est.*	*61.7 est.*	*19 est.*

GROSS TON	NET TON	TYM	DISP
			7300

POWER: BOILER   ENGINE

  10 Water-tube (2 Oil)   *3 Turbines*

BHP (TOTAL)	SPEED (KNOTS)
10,000	

OWNERS:

German Navy as Imperial Yacht

This is somewhat of a mystery vessel. She was certainly under construction, as a grandiloquent successor to the gunboat-appearing Hohenzollern (1893) when World War I commenced. She would have been THE great Royal Yacht as was the intention of her design. There had been, for many years, an intense jealousy of the Kaiser toward his British cousins, especially King Edward VII, who in his easy, confident manner so definitely outshone his ambitious Teutonic cousin. This yacht was projected to have eclipsed the *Victoria and Albert*, *Alexandra*, or any other competitive Royal Yacht.

World War I prevented her completion. After the war, Montague Grahame-White tried to buy her for his fleet of charter yachts. However, she was so far from completion that the deal fell through. Eventually, in an unfinished state, she was sold and broken up in about 1923.

GEM ~ 1913

Other Names
ATHERO
GYPSY JO
CONDOR
CAROLUS
CONDOR

DESIGNER: *Cox & Stevens*
BUILT: *1913* BY *George Lawley*
MATERIAL: *Steel* RIG: *Twin Screw Steamer*

LOA	LWL	BEAM	DRAFT in feet
164.5	153.5	18.0	7.0

GROSS TON	NET TON	TYM	DISP
201	113	226	

POWER: BOILER ENGINE
2 TE 12½ × 19⅜ × 22 × 22/15 each

BHP (TOTAL)	SPEED (KNOTS)
2200	15

OWNERS:
William Ziegler, Jr., 1913–1922
US Navy World War I
Jesse Livermore 1922–1926 (Athero)
Russell A. Alger 1926 (Gypsy Jo)
A. E. Mathews 1926–1935 (Condor)
J. E. Smith 1935 (Carolus)
H. P. van Knauf 1936–1941 (Condor)

Gem was one of the popular, fast commuter steam yachts of her era. Though not as fast or powerful as some Seabury or Herreshoff designs, she was one of the more beautiful and successful of that group of yachts. During World War I she operated in Long Island Sound in experiments with submarine detection. She was also used in experiments with colloidal, coal fuel. I have no data on her activities during World War II, but like some other yachts she was not listed in Lloyd's after that war.

WINCHESTER (4th) ~ 1915

Other Names
RENARD

DESIGNER: *Cox & Stevens*
BUILT: *1915* BY *Bath Iron Works*
MATERIAL: *Steel* RIG: *Twin Screw Steamer*

LOA	LWL	BEAM	DRAFT in feet
225	225	21.0	7.5

GROSS TON	NET TON	TYM	DISP
396	205	479	

POWER: BOILER   ENGINE
    2 Water-tube, Oil   *2 Turbines*

BHP (TOTAL)	SPEED (KNOTS)
7000	31.7

OWNERS:
P. W. Rouss 1915–1927
US Navy World War I
Vincent Astor 1928
Russell A. Alger 1929
Cornelius Vanderbilt 1930–1939
B. P. McCurdy 1940
Canadian Navy World War II (HMCS Renard)
W. N. MacDonald (Margaree S.S. Co.) 1951–1957
  (Renard)

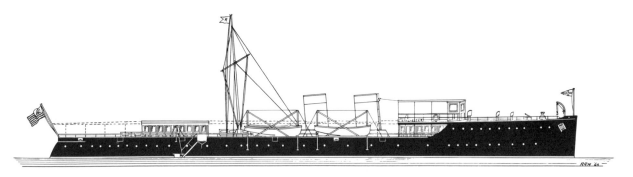

This was the fourth, the largest, the greatest of Peter Rouss's four *Winchesters*. Larger than the third, also designed by Cox & Stevens, she was hard to distinguish from her predecessor. She was built by those masters of destroyer construction, Bath Iron Works in Maine. She was slightly slower than her Yarrow-built predecessor, yet her plan (Fig. 8) shows little increase in owner's accommodations. She evidently satisfied her owner, as, having built three other *Winchesters* in quick succession, he kept this one for the remaining 12 years of his life.

After that Vincent Astor and General Cornelius Vanderbilt owned her. If such experienced yachtsmen owned this *Winchester* one can assume that she was a satisfying yacht.

She served in the Canadian Navy in World War II. After the war she remained in Canada until dropped from Lloyd's after 1956, after more than 30 years of service as a high-speed, lightly constructed yacht, a great tribute to her designer and builders.

HERRESHOFF PATROL BOATS ~ 1917

DESIGNER: *Herreshoff Mfg. Co.*
BUILT: *1917* BY *Herreshoff Mfg. Co.*
MATERIAL: *Steel*   RIG: *Twin Screw Schooner*

LOA	LWL	BEAM	DRAFT in feet
114	*110.3*	*15.3*	*4.7*

GROSS TON	NET TON	TYM	DISP
60			

POWER: BOILER   ENGINE
    Water-Tube   *2 TE 9 × 14 × 22½ /12 each*

BHP (TOTAL)	SPEED (KNOTS)
1200	*20*

OWNERS:
Before turning over to the US Navy were A. I. duPont, R. E. Tod, Payne Whitney, and J. P. Morgan (George Nichols)

After World War I commenced in Europe, many patriots in the United States, including several yachtsmen, were greatly concerned with the lack of combat equipment available in the United States in light of the vast amounts demonstrably required under combat conditions in Europe. Several yachtsmen had built at their own expense patrol craft for presentation to the Navy. Among these were the four yachtsmen listed above who commissioned Herreshoff to build four patrol boats. The principal design work on these boats and engines was done by A. Sidney deW Herreshoff, Capt. Nat's eldest son. Upon completion they were given to the Navy. The four went immediately to Panama, where they formed a defensive patrol force until 1921. Eventually they were sold in 1922 (one of them, SP 1841, for $1366). At least one was converted to a yacht as she was advertised for sale in Yachting in 1928.

ISABEL ~ 1917

DESIGNER: *Cox & Stevens*

BUILT: *1917* BY *Bath Iron Works*

MATERIAL: *Steel* RIG: *Twin Screw Schooner*

LOA	LWL	BEAM	DRAFT in feet
245	230	26	8.6

GROSS TON	NET TON	TYM	DISP
710			930

POWER: BOILER ENGINE

2 Water-tube, Oil *2 Parsons Turbines*

BHP (TOTAL)	SPEED (KNOTS)
8600	28.8

OWNERS:

John N. Willys 1917
US Navy 1917–1946

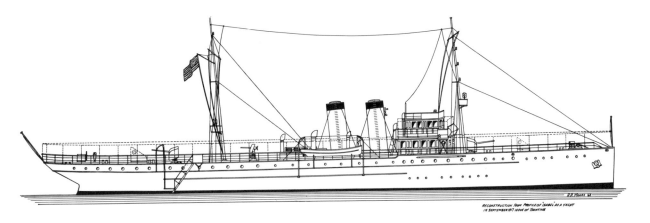

Reconstruction from Profile of Isabel as a Yacht in September 1917 Issue of Yachting

Isabel was ordered by and built for John N. Willys of motor car (and Curtiss Aeroplane) fame, to be the hitherto unobtainable combination of speed, comfort, and seaworthiness. Designed by Cox & Stevens and Bath built, she achieved her goals, but just in time to be sold to the US Navy for $611,553. She was 8–9 knots faster than any contemporary sea-going yacht. Armed with four 3″ guns and four torpedo tubes, she was commissioned not as an armed yacht but as a destroyer, the only yacht so honored.

She went to France and operated there for the duration of the War. After a layup in Philadelphia, she was refitted as a flagship in 1920 and sent to the Asiatic Fleet where she remained as the yacht flag-ship until 1941. Overhauled in Cavite, Philippines, she became a warship again, and dropping back before the Japanese onslaught, she eventually escaped to Australia, after an encounter with a Japanese submarine en route. She served the war in Australian waters becoming a training ship for submarines. After the war she returned to the United States. After 30 years of continual service she was in such worn condition that it was uneconomical to try to put her in serviceable condition again. On February 26, 1946, the gallant *Isabel* was decommissioned and scrapped, a final end for a unique yacht with the normally incompatible characteristics of high speed, seaworthiness, and comfort.

NAVETTE ~ 1917

DESIGNER: *N. G. Herreshoff*
BUILT: *1917* By *Herreshoff Mfg. Co.*
MATERIAL: *Wood*   RIG: *Twin Screw Steamer*

LOA	LWL	BEAM	DRAFT in feet
114	*106*	*14.3*	*3.3*

GROSS TON	NET TON	TYM	DISP
75	*51*		

POWER: BOILER   ENGINE
     1 Water-tube   *2 TE 6 × 10 × 16/9 each*

BHP (TOTAL)	SPEED (KNOTS)
700 est.	*18 est.*

OWNERS:
J. P. Morgan 1917–1934
L. P. Falk 1935
S. H. Stern 1936–1939
W. Warren 1940–1947

Navette was ordered by J. P. Morgan to replace the aging *Mermaid* (ex-*Scout* class *Express* of 1903) as his commuter between New York City and his home on Matinicock Pt. on Long Island Sound. *Navette* was primarily comfortable. She was not as fast as many other commuters of that and later eras, when gasoline powered yachts came into vogue. In 1929 I flew amphibians from East River and 31st Street, and would admire the assembled fleet of yachts awaiting their owners off the New York Yacht Club landing at 26th Street. One by one they would roar away, while in their midst the long lean *Navette* would leave silently and go up river faster than most other commuters, without a sound and hardly a ripple. This was commuting in comfort and in grand style.

After Mr. Morgan sold her she carried on for another 13 years before her last listing in Lloyd's in 1947.

NOKOMIS ~ 1917

DESIGNER: *H. J. Gielow*

BUILT: *1917   By Pusey & Jones, Wilmington,
Delaware*

OWNERS:
H. E. Dodge 1917
US Navy 1917–1944

MATERIAL: *Steel*   RIG: *Twin Screw Schooner*

LOA	LWL	BEAM	DRAFT in feet
243	202	32.0	14.0

GROSS TON	NET TON	TYM	DISP
872	593		

POWER: BOILER   ENGINE
  2 Water-tube, Oil   2 TE 14 × 22½ × 36/24 each

BHP (TOTAL)	SPEED (KNOTS)
	16.25

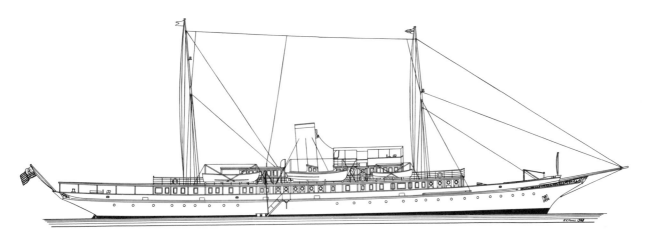

Nokomis was a handsome yacht that upon completion was sold to the Navy before she had been used as a yacht. Commissioned in December, 1917, she served with several other yachts in the Breton Patrol, based in Brest, France. After the war she was retained by the Navy and was a survey ship in the Caribbean for many years. She was laid up in 1938 but was recommissioned in 1942 for further service. She was eventually scrapped in 1944 and broken up for her metal.

UNITED STATES

(1917 as a yacht)

DESIGNER: *Manitowoc SB Co.*

BUILT: *1909*   By *Manitowoc SB Co., Mani-*
towoc Wisconsin

MATERIAL: *Steel*   RIG: *Screw Schooner*

LOA	LWL	BEAM	DRAFT in feet
°256	243	41	15

GROSS TON	NET TON	TYM	DISP
2054			

POWER: BOILER   ENGINE
    3 Scotch   *1 TE 22 × 36½ × 60/40*

BHP (TOTAL)	SPEED (KNOTS)
2500	14.0

° *Lengthened 40' when converted to yacht.*

OWNERS:

Col. E. H. R. Green 1917–1919 (as a yacht)

United States was a passenger-freight vessel on the Great Lakes until purchased and converted for Colonel Green, son of Hetty Green, the famous stock speculator and financier. The conversion was most expensive, but when completed she certainly had extensive accommodations. At about this time, Colonel Green, no longer a young man, married for the first time. His wife did not like boating so the yacht was used only for short coastal trips.

After only two years of use as a yacht, she went ashore in a storm in 1919 from her anchorage off her owner's estate near New Bedford, and was damaged to the extent that it was not considered worthwhile to rebuild her.

CUTTY SARK ~ 1920

DESIGNER: *Yarrow*
BUILT: *1920* BY *Yarrow*
MATERIAL: *Steel*   RIG: *Twin Screw Schooner*

LOA	LWL	BEAM	DRAFT in feet
273	270	25.5	9.0

GROSS TON	NET TON	TYM	DISP
883	339	828	

POWER: BOILER   ENGINE
   Water-tube, Oil   *2 Yarrow Turbines*

BHP (TOTAL)	SPEED (KNOTS)
5000	24

OWNERS:
Major H. Keswick 1920–1926
Duke of Westminster 1927–1939
British Navy World War II

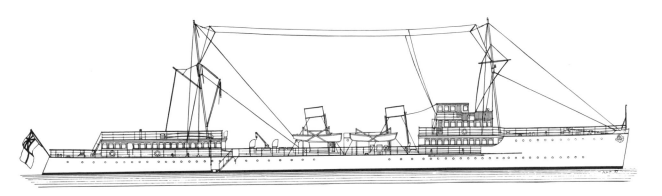

This *Cutty Sark* (not to be confused with the clipper ship) was, even more than the last two *Winchesters*, the nearest approach in appearance to a destroyer of any yacht. The principal difference was her relatively moderate power of 5000 brake horsepower and 24 knots speed compared to the 27,000 brake horsepower and 36 knots speed of contemporary British "R" and "S" class destroyers. It is reputed that her builders, having material on hand to build destroyers subsequently cancelled, built

Cutty Sark. Due to her attractive, racy lines and distinctive appearance, she was a well-known vessel in yachting circles in the United Kingdom between the wars.

She served as a submarine tender during World War II. After the war, she went into commercial service, and as *Joseph Hertz* she smuggled immigrants into Palestine in 1947 and 1948. She is reported to have been scrapped in Britain in 1948 or 1949.

LYNDONIA ~ 1920

DESIGNER: *Consolidated SB Co.*
BUILT: *1920* BY *Consolidated SB Co.*
MATERIAL: *Steel*   RIG: *Twin Screw Schooner*

LOA	LWL	BEAM	DRAFT in feet
230	190	30.0	12.8

GROSS TON	NET TON	TYM	DISP
812	379	824	

POWER: BOILER   ENGINE
   4 Water-tube, Oil *2 TE 12 × 20 ½ × 34/24 each*
                       Changed to Diesel in 1927

BHP (TOTAL)	SPEED (KNOTS)
2000 HP	14½

OWNERS:
C. H. K. Curtis and Mrs. Mary Bok 1920–1940
Pan American Airways 1941–1942 (Southern Seas)
US Navy World War II

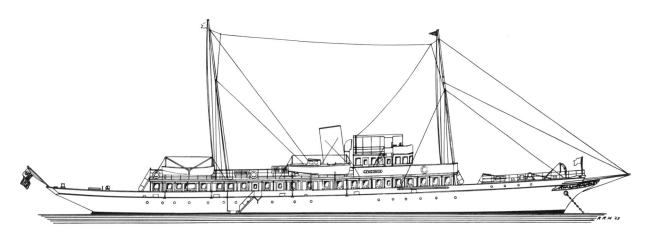

Lyndonia was the first of few yachts powered by steam and built in the United States after World War I. She replaced the pre-war 161' (1906) *Lyndonia* of the same owner. A handsome vessel, she was built by Consolidated S. B. Co., successors to the well-known Gas Engine & Power—Charles L. Seabury Co., many of whose craft have already been listed.

Lyndonia was an expensive yacht as the materials used in her construction, so soon after the war, had been ordered and paid for under expensive wartime conditions. As a yacht, she was owned only by the Curtis/Bok family and most of her cruising was on the Maine Coast, from which her self-made owner came to found and build the Curtis Publishing Co. As the only large yacht based in a small intimate port, Camden, Maine, and as the only large yacht that spent so much of her time in ports around Penobscot Bay, she was well known, and the pride of that part of the coast of Maine. Capt. Albert Rich

and his "down-East" crew helped develop the warm feelings *Lyndonia* enjoyed. After Mr. Curtis died she spent considerable time laid up until in 1940 she was sold to Pan American Airways, who renamed her *Southern Seas*, for service on their transpacific seaplane route. She was bought by the US Engineers as a survey ship but was damaged in grounding in New Caledonia. She was repaired in New Zealand and turned over to the US Navy at the end of 1942 as USS *Southern Seas* (PY 32). She served as a seagoing hotel for officials until she foundered in a typhoon at Okinawa on October 9, 1945. A sad end to a gallant ship.

There has always been some confusion between *Lyndonia* and the 213' yacht *Lydonia*, designed by Gardner and built in 1912 for W. A. Lydon of Chicago. *Lydonia* spent some time on the Great Lakes until taken over first by the US Navy, then by the U.S. Coast & Geodetic Survey as a surveying ship during World War I.

DELPHINE ~ 1921

Other Names
DAUNTLESS

DESIGNER: *H. J. Gielow*
BUILT: *1921* By *Great Lakes Engineering Co.*
MATERIAL: *Steel* RIG: *Twin Screw Schooner*

LOA	LWL	BEAM	DRAFT in feet
258	250	35.5	14.6

GROSS TON	NET TON	TYM	DISP
1286	874	1382	1950

POWER: BOILER   ENGINE
3 Water-tube, Oil   2 QE 14½ × 21 × 30½ × 45/30 each

OWNERS:
H. E. Dodge 1921
Mrs. Delphine Dodge 1922–1968
US Navy World War II (USS Dauntless)
Seafarers International Union 1968 (Dauntless)

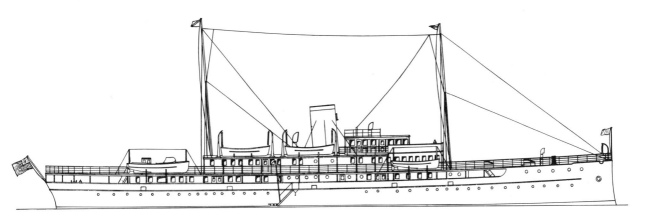

Delphine was built after World War I to replace *Nokomis*, taken over by the Navy in 1917 before the owners could enjoy her as a yacht. *Delphine*, named after Mrs. Dodge, who inherited her on the death of Mr. Dodge, was built on the Great Lakes, and limited in size to the then small Welland Canal locks (These locks and those on the St. Lawrence River were enlarged later on. During World War II numerous 312′ LOA U.S. submarines built on Lake Michigan could not pass the Welland Canal locks bypassing Niagara Falls. Though the route via the Chicago, Illinois, and Mississippi Rivers could take that length, the 17′ draft of the submarines prevented movement under their own power. So a shallow draft lighter-cum-floating drydock was built into which each submarine was floated near Chicago. It was then towed to New Orleans where the submarine resumed its native element and the lighter was returned to await the next completed submarine. During the trip on the rivers, underwater fittings, bearings, etc. were inspected or replaced, and the underbody painted.)

Delphine was used by her owner on the Great Lakes and at times on the New England Coast. In 1927 she caught fire on the Hudson River finally capsizing and sinking. She was completely repaired in 100 days. During World War II she became USS *Dauntless* and served as flagship for Fleet Admiral E. J. King, Chief of Naval Operations. After the war she remained for some years in Detroit, though seldom underway. In 1962 she was laid up in New London, Connecticut, still under her old Captain, W. H. Knight, as caretaker.

In 1968 she was bought by the Seafarers International Union and was to be based at Piney Point, Maryland under the name *Dauntless*.

RESTLESS ~ 1923

Other Names
SANS PEUR
FAISAL I

DESIGNER: *G. L. Watson & Co.*
BUILT: *1923* BY *John Brown, Ltd.*
MATERIAL: *Steel*   RIG: *Twin Screw Schooner*

LOA	LWL	BEAM	DRAFT in feet
203	*186.1*	*29.7*	*13.0*

GROSS TON	NET TON	TYM	DISP
736	*274*	*732*	*1025*

POWER: BOILER   ENGINE
   1 Scotch, Oil *2 TE 12 × 19½ × 22 × 22/20*
                    each

OWNERS:
A. S. Cochran 1923
Lord Tredegar 1924–1926
Duke of Sutherland 1927–1939 (Sans Peur)
Iraq Government 1939– (Faisal I)

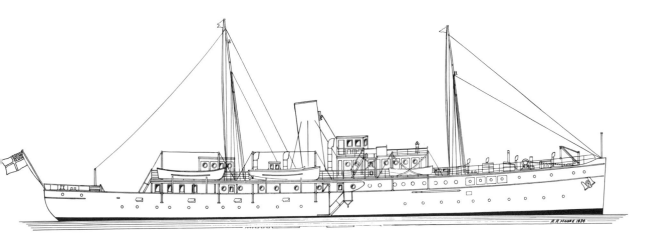

Shortly after her completion, *Restless* made a round-the-world voyage with her ailing owner Alexander Smith Cochran, well known as the former owner of *Westward*, the America's Cup yacht *Vanitie*, the schooner *Sea Call*, the steam yacht *Warrior*, and others.

While owned by the Duke of Sutherland she cruised extensively. Though not as beautiful as some of Watson's former yachts she was extremely comfortable and able. She was sold to the Iraq Government as the Royal Yacht in 1939. Later she became an Iraq lighthouse tender and as late as 1968 was still listed in Jane's.

THALASSA ~ 1924

Other Names
SUILVEN

DESIGNER: *G. L. Watson & Co.*
BUILT: *1924* By *John Brown, Ltd.*
MATERIAL: *Steel*   RIG: *Twin Screw Schooner*

LOA	LWL	BEAM	DRAFT in feet
197	188.8	29.3	13.8

GROSS TON	NET TON	TYM	DISP
876	333	696	

POWER: BOILER   ENGINE
1 Scotch, Oil   2 TE 12 × 19½ × 22 × 22/20 each

BHP (TOTAL)	SPEED (KNOTS)
850 IHP	13

OWNERS:
Eugene Higgins 1924–1939
British Navy World War II
W. G. Hetherington 1948–1949

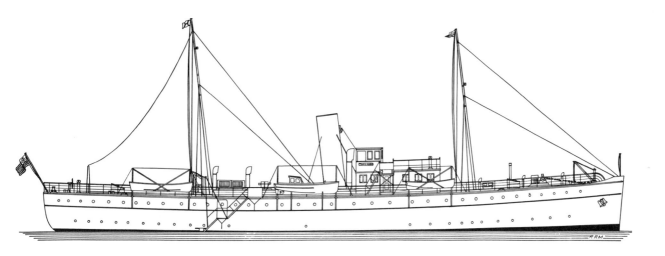

Thalassa was very similar to Restless in appearance, but can be distinguished by her being plated all the way to the stern rather than having Restless's after deckhouse and quarterdeck. Both yachts had the same power plants. Most of her yachting career was spent in European waters. I have heard that she was eventually sold to British Petroleum, Ltd., for use in the Persian Gulf. Like Restless she was a very comfortable, roomy vessel.

KASSED KHEIR ~ 1926

DESIGNED: *Thornycroft*   OWNERS:
BUILT: *1926* By *Thornycoft*   *Egyptian Royal Yacht*
MATERIAL: *Steel*   RIG: *Paddle Schooner*

LOA	LWL	BEAM	DRAFT in feet
237.7	229	32	3.5

GROSS TON	NET TON	TYM	DISP
1330		1111	

POWER: BOILER   ENGINE
                    PADDLE TE 17 × 26 × 43/48
BHP (TOTAL)   SPEED (KNOTS)

This unusual yacht, built by those specialists in shallow draft river warships, was built for the Egyptian Royal Family for service on the shallow waters of the Nile. For this reason she was made a paddle wheeler and was a successful craft for that service. After King Farouk was deposed she served, at least when I visited Cairo in 1958, as an annex to the adjacent Hotel Semiramis.

VIKING ~ 1929

Other Names
NOPARO
USS ST. AUGUSTINE

DESIGNER: *Theodore Wells*
BUILT: *1929* BY *Newport News SB & DD Co.*
MATERIAL: *Steel* RIG: *Twin Screw Schooner*

LOA	LWL	BEAM	DRAFT in feet
272	217.5	36.0	13.0

GROSS TON	NET TON	TYM	DISP
1300	408	1280	

POWER: BOILER ENGINE
   2 Water-tube, Oil   *2 Turbo-electric*

BHP (TOTAL)	SPEED (KNOTS)
2600	16.5

OWNERS:
George F. Baker, Jr. 1929–1937
Norman Woolworth 1938–1940 (Noparo)
US Navy World War II (USS St. Augustine)

242

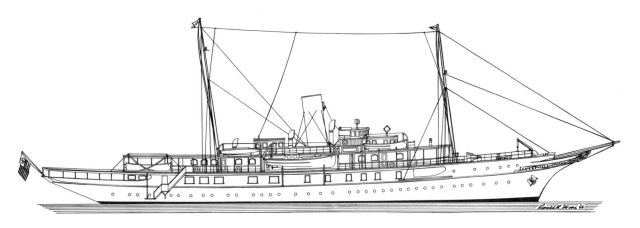

Viking was built to replace an older *Viking*. She was one of the most comfortable, roomy, seaworthy yachts ever built. Her turbo-electric drive gave her smooth, quiet performance, with exceptionable maneuverability. Note the large windows with steel shutters containing deadlights that could be closed in a seaway, yet gave good light under calm conditions. Her owner was an ardent deep-sea fisherman, and *Viking* for nearly eight years followed the fish, going out of commission only in January and February for a few weeks' maintenance and overhaul. Summers she would go to New England, Nova Scotia, and the St. Lawrence, winters to the West Indies, the Galapagos, and the west coast of South America. Fall and spring she would often go to the Mediterranean. Hew owner died in Honolulu during a round-the-world cruise. (Once someone asked Mr. Baker's father how his son could afford such a large expensive yacht whereas his own vessel was quite small. Mr. Baker Sr.'s reply was, "He has a rich father.")

During the war she became the USS *St. Augustine* but was sunk in a collision off Cape May, New Jersey, in January, 1944.

As mentioned above Mr. Baker had a previous *Viking*, T. E. Wells design, built in 1909 by Pusey & Jones. She was 180' LOA. Her name was changed to *Falcon* when the new *Viking* was built.

CORSAIR (4th) ~ 1930

DESIGNER: *H. J. Gielow*
BUILT: *1930* By *Bath Iron Works*
MATERIAL: *Steel* RIG: *Twin Screw Schooner*

LOA	LWL	BEAM	DRAFT in feet
343.5	280	42.7	18.0

GROSS TON	NET TON	TYM	DISP
2142	470	2653	

POWER: BOILER ENGINE
   4 Water-tube, Oil   *2 GE Turbo-electric*

BHP (TOTAL)	SPEED (KNOTS)
6000	17

OWNERS:
J. P. Morgan 1930–1940
British Navy World War II
Commercial interests 1946–1949

244

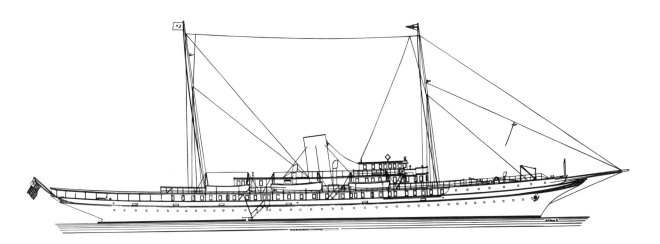

This, the fourth of the great family of *Corsairs*, replaced that splendid *Corsair* (3rd) after 31 years of service. Probably no two men had had more experience with large yachts than had her owner, J. P. Morgan, and her captain, W. B. Porter. The result of their planning was one of the most nearly perfect privately owned craft ever developed. It can truly be said that she was the crown at the end of the steam yacht era. Already most yachts were by then diesel powered. *Corsair*, like *Viking*, had turbo-electric power combining smoothness, silence, and exceptional maneuvering ability. Her plans, shown in the text as Fig. 7, show a layout developed after many years of experience and use.

After only ten years of use, mainly in the United States east coast and in the West Indies, she was turned over to the British Navy for service during World War II. After the war she was completely overhauled and fitted out as a deluxe cruise ship for service on the West Coast. In summers she cruised to Alaskan waters, while in winters she went south to Acapulco, Mexico. She was wrecked off Acapulco on November 12, 1949, and beached outside that harbor.

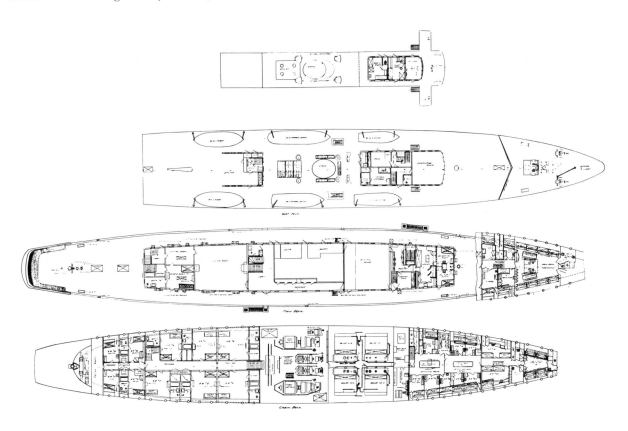

NAHLIN ~ 1930

Other Names
LUCEAFARUL
LIBERATATEA

DESIGNER: *G. L. Watson & Co.*
BUILT: *1930* BY *John Brown, Ltd.*
MATERIAL: *Steel* RIG: *Twin Screw Schooner*

LOA	LWL	BEAM	DRAFT in feet
300	250	36.0	14.8

GROSS TON	NET TON	TYM	DISP
1391	556	1574	

POWER: BOILER ENGINE
  2 Water-tube, Oil *2 Geared Turbines*

BHP (TOTAL)	SPEED (KNOTS)
4000	17.4

OWNERS
Lady Yule 1930–1937
Roumanian Government 1937 as Royal Yacht and later school ship

While *Corsair* was the ultimate in steam yachts in the United States, *Nahlin* was probably her opposite in the United Kingdom. As in the case of *Corsair*, nearly all her contemporaries were diesel powered. *Nahlin's* owner was the widow of a banker with Indian interests. She had evidently wished to travel extensively, so in *Nahlin* her wish was granted. For four years she cruised continually, covering over 200,000 miles and visiting all European waters, the Central Atlantic, the West Indies and Gulf of Mexico, to the Galapagos, up the West Coast to California, Hawaii to Tahiti and intervening islands, New Zealand, and Australia. Finally her owner, deciding she had visited all the places she wished to see, made

little use of *Nahlin*, which was frequently under charter. The best known of these charters was probably that to the ex-Prince of Wales, shortly after he became King Edward VIII. Among the several guests on this cruise on the Mediterranean, which was extensively covered in the press, was Mrs. Simpson, the present Duchess of Windsor, his wife.

Nahlin was the last steam yacht designed by that most experienced firm of Watson. Her plans (Fig. 6) are given to show the state of the art at that time. She was sold to the Roumanian Government as the private yacht for King Carol. She later became a school ship. She is still in use, though when seen in Galata in 1967, she appeared somewhat neglected.

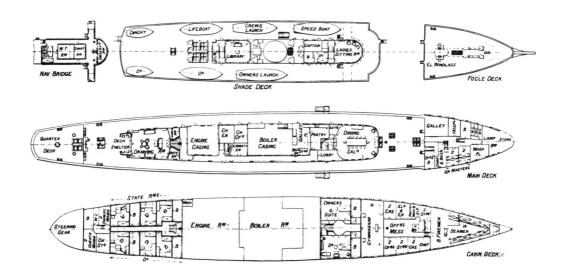

ROVER ~ 1930

Other Names

SOUTHERN CROSS
ORIZABA
ZARAGOZA

DESIGNER: *Alexander Stephen & Sons*
BUILT: *1930* BY *Alexander Stephen & Sons*
MATERIAL: *Steel*   RIG: *Twin Screw Schooner*

LOA	LWL	BEAM	DRAFT in feet
320	*260*	*40.0*	*15.0*

GROSS TON	NET TON	TYM	DISP
1881	*734*	*2118*	*1851*

POWER: BOILER   ENGINE
    3 Scotch, Oil   *2 QE 16½ × 27½ × 32½*
                            × 32½/30 each

BHP (TOTAL)   SPEED (KNOTS)
    2600

OWNERS
Lord Inchcape 1930–1932
Rover SS Corp. (Howard Hughes) 1933–1937
    (Southern Cross)
Alex Wenner-Gren 1938–1939
Mexican Navy 1939–1960 (Orizaba)

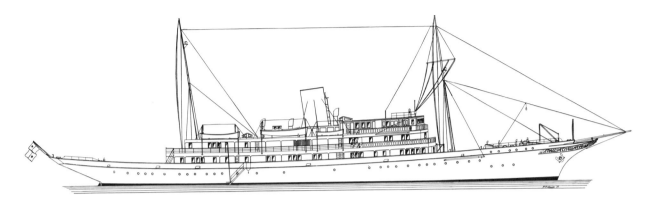

It is said that Lord Inchcape, head of the vast P & O shipping group, while on a voyage to the Orient, cabled Alexander Stephens to build him a 2000 ton, reciprocating-engined steam yacht and to start construction at once. Delighted with such an order, the yard took the precaution to insure that the cable was not a hoax by calling on the P & O office in London. They were told that if Lord Inchcape had cabled them to build a yacht, he meant it. So her construction was well under way when he returned. An experienced shipping man, he put his trust in Scotch boilers and "up-and-down" engines, so *Rover* was rather old-fashioned compared to other contemporary yachts. Her owner's daughter, the Honorable Elsie Mackay, had been lost on an attempted transatlantic flight in 1928, so *Rover's* figurehead was supposedly of her.

She was sold through Herbert Julyan to an unknown American client who turned out to be Howard Hughes. Her new owner with his many interests, particularily aviation, seldom used her, so she was sold to Alex Wenner-Gren, the Swedish industrialist, in 1938. She was in the Atlantic when World War II began and became headline news when she rescued many of the passengers and crew from the liner *Athenia*, torpedoed and sunk without warning on September 3, 1939.

Later she is supposed to have taken Spanish Republican gold to Mexico. In any case she went into the Mexican Navy as a training ship, in which service she remained until scrapped about 1960.

XARIFA ~ 1930

Other Names
HMS BLACK BEAR
CAYMANIA

DESIGNER: *J. M. Soper*
BUILT: *1930* By *J. Samuel White, Cowes*
MATERIAL: *Steel*   RIG: *Twin Screw Schooner*

LOA	LWL	BEAM	DRAFT in feet
204.4	166	31.1	13

GROSS TON	NET TON	TYM	DISP
731	330	756	

POWER: BOILER   ENGINE
        1 Scotch, Oil   *2 TE 11¾ × 18 × 29/24 each*
BHP (TOTAL)   SPEED (KNOTS)

OWNERS:
F. M. Singer 1930–1947
British Navy World War II
Commerical interests 1951–

250

Xarifa, with her Maierform-type bow, was a distinctive yacht, seaworthy and comfortable.

She served in the Trinidad area during the war and after was bought for service to the Cayman Islands and Jamaica as *SS Caymania*.

ROUSSALKA ~ 1931

(1931 as a yacht)

Other Names
SS BRIGHTON (as cross-channel steamer)

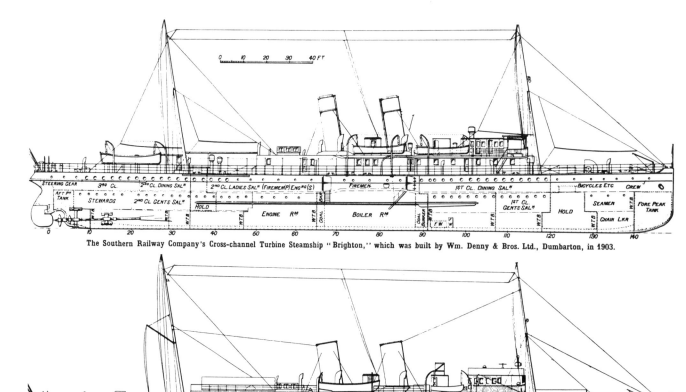

The Southern Railway Company's Cross-channel Turbine Steamship "Brighton," which was built by Wm. Denny & Bros. Ltd., Dumbarton, in 1903.

DESIGNER: *Denny*
BUILT: *1905* BY *Wm. Denny as Steamer, Conv. 1931*
MATERIAL: *Steel*   RIG: *Triple Screw Schooner*
LOA   LWL   BEAM   DRAFT in feet
                          34.2
GROSS TON   NET TON   TYM   DISP
1433   592   1489
POWER: BOILER   ENGINE
  2 Scotch (Oil in 1931)   3 Parsons Turbines
BHP (TOTAL)   SPEED (KNOTS)

OWNERS:
Sir Walter Guinness (Lord Moyne after 1933) 1931–1933 (as yacht)

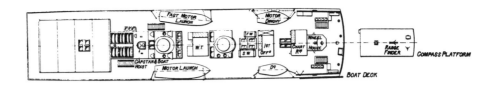

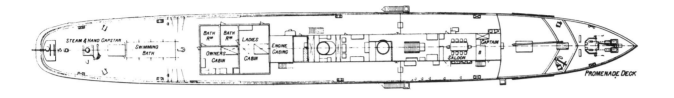

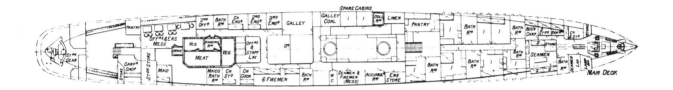

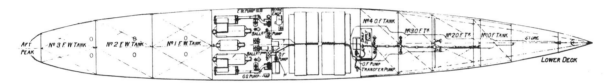

Sir Walter Guinness had admired the British cross-channel steamers and felt they could be converted to fast, roomy yachts. His first conversion was of SS *Canterbury* (Denny, 1901) into the yacht *Arpha* in 1927. Mr. L. N. Hire at about the same time had the SS *Folkstone* (Denny, 1903) converted into the yacht *Solway*, which was broken up in 1936. Sir Walter Guinness sold *Arpha* (which was dropped from Lloyd's in 1938) and bought the turbine powered SS *Brighton* (Denny, 1905) and converted her into the yacht *Roussalka*. Her plans before and after conversion show what can be done. Unfortunately she was lost off the coast of Ireland in August, 1933. Her owner then bought the SS *Dieppe* (Fairfield, 1905) and converted her to the yacht *Rosaura*. During this conversion in 1934 her steam plant was removed and replaced by diesels. While on war service she was sunk in April 1941.

SAVARONA (3rd) ~ 1931

Other Names
GUNES DIL

DESIGNER: *Gibbs & Cox*
BUILT: *1931* By *Blohm & Voss*
MATERIAL: *Steel*   RIG: *Twin Screw Schooner*

LOA	LWL	BEAM	DRAFT in feet
408.5	350	53.0	20.5

GROSS TON	NET TON	TYM	DISP
4646	1501	4677	

POWER: BOILER   ENGINE
    4 Water-tube, Oil   *2 Geared Turbines*

BHP (TOTAL)	SPEED (KNOTS)
10750	21

OWNERS:
Mrs. E. R. Cadwalader 1931–1938
Turkish Government 1938– (Gunes Dil, name seldom used)

254

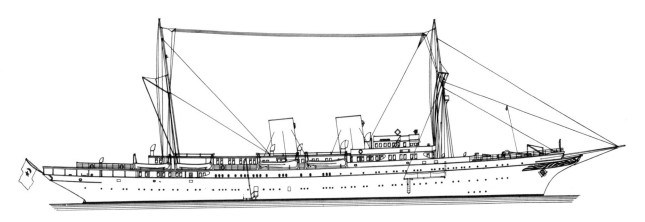

Savarona, third of that name built for Mrs. Cadwalader, was the most expensive, probably the most luxurious, and certainly the largest non-royal yacht ever built. Everything about her drew superlatives. Her cost was reported to have been over four million dollars. She had a crew of 83 with a payroll estimated to be about $250,000 per year. Her bare charter fee was at one time reported to be $80,000 per month, to which expenses of wages, fuel, food, and supplies had to be added.

Built in Germany, the import duties into the United States would have been so great that she remained under a flag of convenience and never came closer to the United States than Bermuda. Her owner used her only two seasons. Thereafter she remained idle or available for charter until she was bought by the Turkish Government in 1938 as the yacht for Kemel Ataturk for a reputed one million dollars. She was supposed to have been called *Gunes Dil* but the name *Savarona* seems to have been retained and used instead. After the President's death, she eventually went into the Turkish Navy as a school ship, in which service she remains to date.

GRILLE ~ 1934

DESIGNER: *German Admiralty*
BUILT: *1934*   BY *Blohm & Voss*
MATERIAL: *Steel*   RIG: *Twin Screw Schooner*

LOA	LWL	BEAM	DRAFT in feet
377.3	326	44.3	11.3

GROSS TON	NET TON	TYM	DISP
3378	1082		2560

POWER: BOILER   ENGINE
   Water-tube, Oil   *2 Geared Turbines*

BHP (TOTAL)	SPEED (KNOTS)
22000	26

OWNERS:
German Navy
British Navy as reparations
George Arida

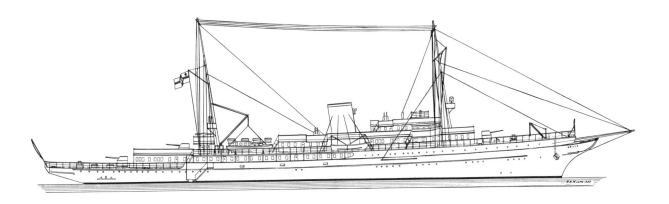

Grille, a handsome craft, was built for the German Navy and classed as a dispatch boat. In these days of radio and other electronic communications devices the task of a dispatch boat is, to say the least, redundant, except to serve as a conveniently established category into which a vessel desired for other purposes can be classified. *Grille* served as the Admiralty yacht and as such was often used to demonstrate to and to educate political party officials, whose rapid growth to power was strongly influenced by the army and air force, as to the desirability and need for a large and strong navy.

During World War II she served as a mine-layer and later as a training ship before becoming the flag-ship of the Admiral, North Sea Command. On May 1, 1945, Admiral Doenitz proclaimed Hitler's death from the *Grille*. Taken by the British in reparations she was sold to a George Arida, a Lebanese textile manufacturer who took her to the United States. It was found too costly to put her in shape to use or to charter, so she was finally scrapped at Bordentown, New Jersey in 1949.

A previous *Grille* was designed and built by Normand of Le Havre in 1856 for the then King of Prussia, later Emperor of Germany. She was 187' LOA and of 326 gross tons. She lasted as a fishery protective vessel and school ship until broken up after World War I.

BRITANNIA ~ 1954

DESIGNER: *British Admiralty*
BUILT: 1954 By *John Brown, Ltd.*
MATERIAL: *Steel*   RIG: *Twin Screw Schooner*

LOA	LWL	BEAM	DRAFT in feet
412.3	380	55.0	15.6

GROSS TON	NET TON	TYM	DISP
5769	2370	5111	4715

POWER: BOILER   ENGINE
   2 Water-tube, Oil   2 Geared Turbines

BHP (TOTAL)	SPEED (KNOTS)
12000	22.75

OWNERS:
British Navy as Royal Yacht

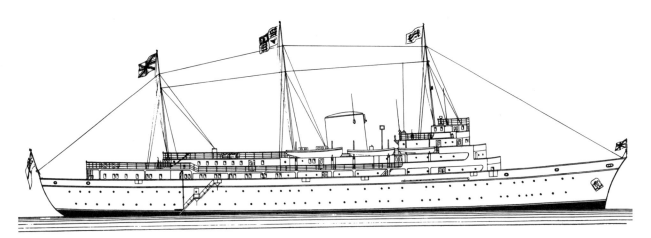

Britannia was built to replace the aged (37 year) *Victoria and Albert* as the British Royal Yacht. Such a yacht was needed at least in the opinion of some people, but strongly objected to by others as squandering of public funds. The preliminary designs of the new yacht were developed as far back as 1939. They lay dormant during the war and subsequent reconstruction period. In 1951, doctors, concerned with the health of King George VI, recommended relaxing sea voyages. As a justification for such expenditures, the designs incorporated complete and quick change from a royal yacht to a naval hospital ship. John Brown, experienced in yacht construction, was selected as the builder. She was commissioned on January 11, 1954. Though modern in appearance, she retains the three masts of former Royal Yachts permitting the simultaneous display, when the monarch is aboard, of the Lord High Admiral's flag at the fore, the Royal Standard at the main, and the Union Jack at the mizzen.

Britannia is turbine powered and is fitted with stabilizers. Her interior can be described as conservatively modern. A special bridge for the Royal Family is incorporated forward of the navigational bridge.

Since commissioning, *Britannia* has made extensive cruises with the Royal Family, often going out to arrive on station while the Family save time by flying out and back. She has often been used by the Duke of Edinburgh to make visits to many distant and, in the opinion of some people, minor parts of the Empire where heretofore no member of the Royal Family has ever visited. Such visits have given much pride and pleasure in remote places.

CHRISTINA ~ 1954

Other Names
HMCS STORMONT

DESIGNER:
BUILT: *1943* By *Canadian Vickers*
        1954   (as yacht) Howaldswerke
MATERIAL: *Steel*   RIG: *Twin Screw Schooner*
LOA   LWL   BEAM   DRAFT in feet
325.3   *295*   *36.5*   *15.2*
GROSS TON   NET TON   TYM   DISP
  1602   *739*   *1724*
POWER: BOILER   ENGINE
  2 Water-tube, Oil   2 TE 18½ × 31 × 38½ ×
                        38½/30 each
BHP (TOTAL)   SPEED (KNOTS)
  6500   *21*

OWNERS
Aristotle Onassis 1954–

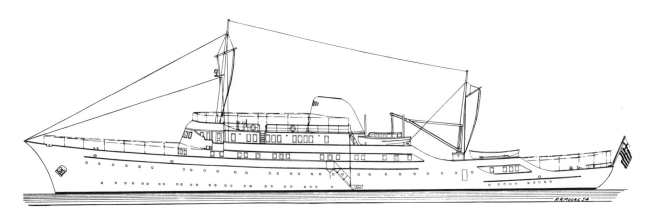

Christina's hull was that of a Canadian-built River class of frigate, one of a large class built in Canada and the United States for anti-submarine convoy work. All became surplus when the war ended. Onassis, the Argentine-Greek shipowner, had her converted to what is, at least in this era, the most luxurious yacht in service. She carries an amphibian airplane, and was one of the first vessels fitted with Vosper anti-rolling stabilizers. The floor of her swimming pool on deck can be set at any level from that of a diving pool, through a wading pool, to become level with the deck as a dance floor.

Another wartime frigate, USS *Natchez*, or HMCS *Annam*, was also converted into the yacht *Moineau* in 1952, owned by Mme. Lucienne Benitez-Rexach of the Dominican Republic. Madame Benitez-Rexach was formerly the well-known French actress called Moineau. This yacht has been advertised for sale for a number of years recently.

PICTURE CREDITS

Warrior 1904
Agawa 1907
Winchester 1907
Cassandra 1908
Iolanda 1908
Little Sovereign 1909
Winchester 1909
Winchester 1912
Cyprus 1913
United States 1917
Lyndonia 1920
Delphine 1921
Viking 1929

R. R. MOORE   *Courtesy of*
Ballymena 1888
Vamoose 1890
Clermont 1892
Lorena 1903
Wakiva II 1907
Triad 1909
Nokomis 1917

NEW YORK YACHT CLUB
    Courtesy of
Corsair 1880
Electra 1884
Say When 1888
Eleanor 1894
Sovereign 1896
Tuscarora 1897
Atmah 1898
Banshee 1900
Arrow 1902
Sovereign 1911

A & J PAVIA MALTA   *Photo by*
Mahroussa 1865

PEABODY MUSEUM   *Courtesy of*
Corsair 1890

M. ROSENFELD & SONS
    Photo by
Scout 1899
Lysistrata 1900
Hauoli 1903
Niagara IV 1903
Alcyone 1907

Vanadis 1908
Navette 1917
Savarona 1931
Cassandra's Crew
Niagara's Library

RUDDER   *Courtesy of*
Kanahwa overhauling others
Sovereign 1911
North Star 1853

SHIP BUILDING & SHIPPING RECORD
    Drawings by
Roussalka

STEBBINS COLLECTION SPNEA
    Courtesy of
Victoria and Albert 1855
Winchester 1915

U.S. COAST GUARD   *Photo by*
Mayflower

U.S. LIBRARY OF CONGRESS
    Courtesy of
Namouna 1882

U.S. NAVY   *Photo by*
Stiletto 1885 as torpedo boat
Cleopatra 1893
Mayflower 1897
Isabel 1917
Herreshoff Patrol boats 1917

UPPER CLYDE S. B. LTD
    Photo by
Doris 1910

VOSPER-THORNYCROFT
    Courtesy of
Kassed Kheir 1926

G. L. WATSON & CO.
    Courtesy of
Veglia 1895
Margarita 1896
Nahma 1897
Varuna 1897
Victoria and Albert 1899
Margarita 1900
Honor 1905

BIBLIOGRAPHY

American Naval Fighting Ships, Vol. I, II, III. U.S. Navy Dept. Government Printing Office

Anderson, Isabel, *A Cruise in the Mediterranean on Sayonara*. Marshall Jones, 1930

Atkins, J. B., *Further Memorials of the Royal Yacht Squadron*. Goffrey Bles, 1939

Baader, Juan, *Cruceros Lanchas Veloces*. Nautica Baader, 1951

Baker, W. A., *The Engine Powered Vessel*. Grosset & Dunlap, 1965

The Book of Sport, pub. J. F. Taylor, 1901 (Articles by W. P. Stephens, I. Cox)

Brassey, Earl, *Sunbeam RYS*. John Murray, 1918

Brassey, Mrs., *A Voyage in the Sunbeam*. Henry Holt & Co., 1888

Brassey, Mrs., *Sunshine & Storm in the East*. Longmans Green, 1881

British Yachts and Yachtsmen. The Yachtsman, 1907

Broughton, V., *Desultory (More desultory) Notes at Sea*. Privately published

Choules, *Cruise of the North Star*. Gould & Lincoln, 1854

Cozzens, F. S., *Yachts & Yachting*. Cassell & Co., 1887 (Chapter by E. S. Jaffrey)

Crane, Clinton, *Clinton Crane's Yachting Memories*. D. Van Nostrand Co. 1952

Eskew, G. L., *Cradle of Ships—History of Bath Iron Works*. Putnam, 1956

Gavin, C. M., *Royal Yachts*. Rich & Cowan, Ltd., 1932

Graham-White, M., *At the Wheel Ashore and Afloat*.

Guest & Bolton, *Memorials of the Royal Yacht Squadron*. John Murray, 1903

Heckstall-Smith and Hope, *Dixon Kemps Manual of Yacht and Boat Sailing and Architecture*. Horace Cox, 1913

Heckstall-Smith, A., *Sacred Cowes*. Anthony Blond, Ltd., 1965

Herreshoff, L. Francis, *Capt. Nat Herreshoff*. Sheridan House, 1953

Herreshoff, L. Francis, *Introduction to Yachting*. Sheridan House, 1963

Heyl, Erik, *Early American Steamers*, 3 vols.

History of American Yachts & Yachtsmen, Spirit of the Times, 1901

Howell, G. F., *Steam Vessels & Marine Engines*. The American Shipbuilder, 1896

Hughes, John Scott, *Famous Yachts*. Methuen & Co., 1928

Hughes, John Scott, *Sailing Through Life*. Methuen & Co., 1947

Julyan, Herbert, *Sixty Years of Yachts*. Hutchinson

Kunhardt, C. P., *Steam Yachts and Launches*. Forest & Stream, 1887

McAdam, Roger, *Salts of the Sound*. Stephen Daye Press, 1957

McAdam, Roger, *The Old Fall River Line*. Stephen Daye Press, 1955

Mott, *Yachts & Yachtsmen of America*. International Yacht Publishing Co., 1894

Paine, R. D., *Corsair in the War Zone*. 1919

Plant, M. F., *Cruise of the Iolanda*. G. P. Putnam & Sons, 1911

SAE Journal 1962, Modern Automotive Steam Power Plant. Dooley, Bell

Talbot-Booth, E. C. *Yachts, Yachting & Sailing*. 1938

Taylor, W. H. and Rosenfeld, Stanley, *The Story of American Yachting*. Appleton Century Crofts, 1958

Vogel, Karl, *Aloha around the World*. G. P. Putnam & Sons, 1922

Wallace, William N., *The Macmillan Book of Boating*. Macmillan, 1964

Winchester, C., *Shipping Wonders of the World*, Vol. I & II. The Amalgamated Press Ltd., London

Jane's All the World's Fighting Ships
Lloyd's Register of American Yachts New York
Lloyd's Register of Yachts London
Rudder
Yachting
Yachting Monthly
Yachting World
The Yachtsman

INDEX

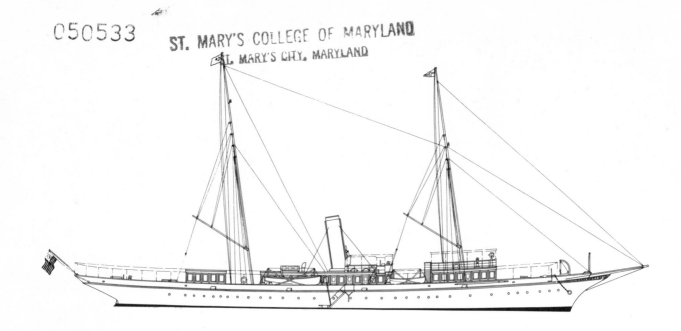

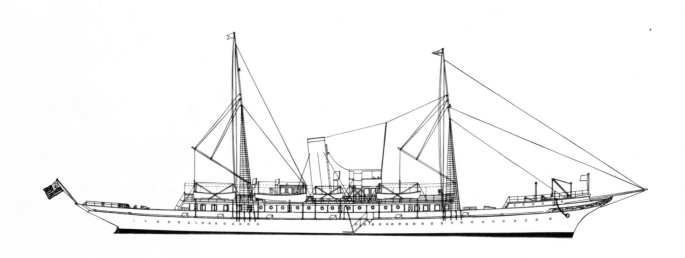

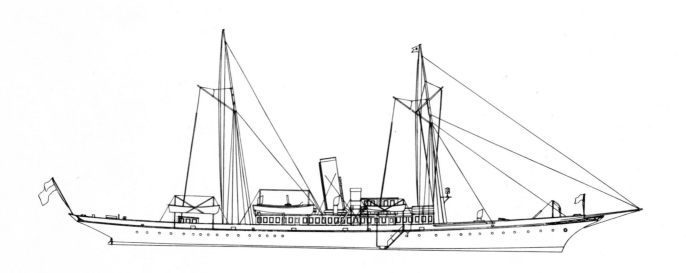